Global University Rankings and the Mediatization of Higher Education

Palgrave Studies in Global Higher Education

Series Editors: **Roger King**, School of Management, University of Bath, UK; **Jenny Lee**, Centre for the Study of Higher Education, University of Arizona, USA; **Simon Marginson**, Institute of Education, University of London, UK; **Rajani Naidoo**, School of Management, University of Bath, UK

This series aims to explore the globalization of higher education and the impact this has had on education systems around the world, including East Asia, Africa, the Middle East, Europe and the US. Analyzing HE systems and policy, this series will provide a comprehensive overview of how HE within different nations and/ or regions is responding to the new age of universal mass higher education.

Titles include:

Michael Dobbins and Christoph Knill
HIGHER EDUCATION GOVERNANCE AND POLICY CHANGE IN WESTERN EUROPE
International Challenges to Historical Institutions

Christof Van Mol
INTRA-EUROPEAN STUDENT MOBILITY IN INTERNATIONAL HIGHER EDUCATION CIRCUITS
Europe on the Move

Lý Trần, Simon Marginson, Hoàng Đỗ, Quyên Đỗ, Trúc Lê, Nhài Nguyễn, Thảo Vũ, Thạch Phạm and Hương Nguyễn
HIGHER EDUCATION IN VIETNAM
Flexibility, Mobility and Practicality in the Global Knowledge Economy

Zinaida Fadeeva, Laima Galkute, Clemens Mader and Geoff Scott (*editors*)
SUSTAINABLE DEVELOPMENT AND QUALITY ASSURANCE IN HIGHER EDUCATION
Transformation of Learning and Society

Maria Yudkevich, Philip G. Altbach and Laura E. Rumbley (*editors*)
ACADEMIC INBREEDING AND MOBILITY IN HIGHER EDUCATION
Global Perspectives

Palgrave Studies in Global Higher Education
Series Standing Order ISBN 978–1–137–34814–2 Hardback
(*outside North America only*)

You can receive future titles in this series as they are published by placing a standing order. Please contact your bookseller or, in case of difficulty, write to us at the address below with your name and address, the title of the series and the ISBN quoted above.

Customer Services Department, Macmillan Distribution Ltd, Houndmills, Basingstoke, Hampshire RG21 6XS, England

Global University Rankings and the Mediatization of Higher Education

Michelle Stack
University of British Columbia, Canada

First published 2016 by
PALGRAVE MACMILLAN

Palgrave Macmillan in the UK is an imprint of Macmillan Publishers Limited, registered in England, company number 785998, of Houndmills, Basingstoke, Hampshire RG21 6XS.

Palgrave Macmillan in the US is a division of St Martin's Press LLC, 175 Fifth Avenue, New York, NY 10010.

Palgrave Macmillan is the global academic imprint of the above companies and has companies and representatives throughout the world.

Palgrave® and Macmillan® are registered trademarks in the United States, the United Kingdom, Europe and other countries.

ISBN: 978–1–137–47594–7

This book is printed on paper suitable for recycling and made from fully managed and sustained forest sources. Logging, pulping and manufacturing processes are expected to conform to the environmental regulations of the country of origin.

A catalogue record for this book is available from the British Library.

Library of Congress Cataloging-in-Publication Data

Stack, Michelle, 1967–
Global university rankings and the mediatization of higher education / Michelle Stack, University of British Columbia, Canada.
    pages cm—(Palgrave studies in global higher education)
Includes index.
ISBN 978–1–137–47594–7
    1. Universities and colleges – Ratings and rankings. 2. Education, Higher – Marketing. I. Title.
LB2331.62.S72 2015
378—dc23   2015025929

To David Perry, my spouse, who has stuck with me through four degrees, tenure and promotion, and various trials and tribulations. Thank you for the "care and feeding of your academic," your sense of humor and commitment to a more equitable and just world. Thank you also for reminding me, when needed, what a privilege it is to be paid to teach and learn from committed and brilliant students, work with insightful and wise colleagues, and do research I'm passionate about.

Contents

Acknowledgments

The work of academics is sometimes represented as solitary, but ideas, encouragement and mentorship are dependent on the generosity of others, and many people have shown me great generosity. The University of British Columbia (UBC) where I work is on unceded and ancestral lands of the Musqueam First Nation. I am thankful to the Musqueam for being so welcoming and generous in educating settlers and visitors including me about their territory.

Thankfully, many years ago André Mazawi and I started our jobs at UBC on the same day. He has been a steadfast friend and exceptional mentor and spent many hours discussing this book with me. Thank you to Suher Zaher-Mazawi who was the indexer for this book and a wonderful friend. Thank you to David Coulter who went over the final draft of this manuscript and provided extensive and exceptionally helpful assistance. I am also thankful to David for predictably asking "what makes for a good and worthwhile education?" It is a foundational question that often gets forgotten. I also owe special thanks to Mary Lynn Young for her mentorship and friendship, as well as for being a great editor and for compassionately prodding me to write this book. I would like to thank Deirdre Kelly for her mentorship and for inviting me to her class to present the chapter on the Times Higher Education rankings. Quinn Kelly, thank you for your valiant attempts to teach me how to draw comics and keep me grounded in a reality that does not involve rankings. I am grateful to Jo-Ann Archibald for the profound teachings she so generously shares on Indigenous ways of thinking about knowledge and responsibility.

Thank you to Leticia Pamela Garcia and Yu Guo, who with aplomb collected website data and coded it; to Hong Lai (Catherine) for early discussions about the ARWU rankings based on her graduating paper and to the senior staff members of public affairs who took time out of their busy schedules to share their expertise with me.

I would like to thank Shauna Butterwick, whom I admire as a scholar and activist and who always has such generosity in providing feedback and great accessories, too! Just as I was in danger of becoming complacent Hartej Gill arrived. I thank her for her courageous challenges to institutional injustice and her invitation to join with others to advocate for a better world. Thank you to Michelle Pidgeon, who first invited me to present at a higher education conference on my initial work around rankings, which eventually led to this project.

I would like to thank Don Fisher for always providing encouragement and places to present my work for feedback, in particular UBC's Center for Higher Education and Training; Chris Gratham, doctoral student and also a professor, for providing the impetus to read more about HE and markets – he also got me thinking about the metaphor of choreography in understanding policy; and Ali Abdi, for his helpful feedback on my concluding chapter.

Thank you to Amy Benson Brown, an amazing editor, for helping me figure out what I really wanted to say in this book; to Alison Mustard, an amazingly efficient and accurate transcriptionist; to Andrew James and Eleanor Christie from Palgrave Macmillan for approaching me to write a book and for keeping me on track to complete this book in a timely manner.

Thank you to Shan Hongxia for joining me on a writing retreat and for her generosity in sharing ideas, food and humor; I look forward to having more time for walks and tea. I would also like to thank Tamam, Sobhi, Kenza and Maleekah for their friendship and for the delicious creation of my favorite Vancouver restaurant – Tamam Fine Palestinian Restaurant.

Thank you to Frank and Danse Williams for sharing their talents as carvers and reminding me, as Danse says, "In my culture if you stop learning you are dead".

Special thanks to Candis Callison and Kathryn Gretsinger for their thought-provoking conversations about communicating academic research to diverse audiences.

Last but least, thank you to Claire Theaker-Brown, Maureen and Diane Brown for being a long-standing, and at times long-suffering, fabulous cheerleading squad. I am grateful to my mother, Yvette Stack, for encouraging me to be skeptical of things that seemed too good to be true and to do my own research.

I of course take all responsibility for any errors in the following work.

Glossary

ARWU   Academic Ranking of World Universities, also called the Shanghai Ranking. It was the first of the "Big Three rankings."

The Big Three refers to the ARWU, QS and THEWUR rankings.

BRICS   Brazil, Russia, India, China and South Africa. THEWUR and QS developed a separate BRICS ranking.

Elsevier owns Scopus, ScienceDirect, and a number of journals.

HEI   Higher Educational Institutions

IREG   International Ranking Expert Group – was formed to evaluate and certify rankings. The IREG advisory includes representatives from major rankings, academics and consultants.

ISI   Institute for Scientific Information was a citation management system developed by Eugene Garfield in the 1960s. It was bought by Thomson in 1992 and became Thomson ISI; now it is called the Web of Science. It is part of Thomson Reuters' suite of intellectual property and business products.

QS   Quacquarelli Symonds was founded in 1990. Nunzio Quacquarelli is the managing director of QS. The company provides software services to universities for monitoring and benchmarking, as well as consulting services; they have a number of products related to business education, including a world MBA tour.

Scopus   Owned by Elsevier, this is a large citation index used for 2014–2015 Times Higher Education ranking and other rankings.

Shanghai Consultancy is associated with the ARWU ranking.

THES   The Times Higher Education Supplement is owned by TES.

THEWUR   The Times Higher Education World University Rankings, sometimes referred to as THE ranking or THES ranking.

TPG Capital owns TES and has $70.2 billion of capital under its management. (1)

TSL Education Group Ltd owns TES Connect, THEWUR. http://www.
bloomberg.com/profiles/companies/8393052Z:LN-tsl-education-
group-ltd.

WOS   Web of Science, previously called Web of Knowledge. It
            is owned by Thomson Reuters and is a citation indexing
            service; it continues to be used by a number of rankings to
            determine the research productivity ranking of universities.

Introduction

Rankings are not passive instruments; nor do they convey neutral messages. They actively reshape narratives of and about higher education. They refigure discursive spaces of what it means to be a university, and a "good" one at that. Within these spaces there is need for active contestation – for debate to expand beyond the measurable to the broader issues of what is a good and worthwhile education in both local and global contexts. I hope this book will be of use to students and parents looking at higher education options, to media and policymakers wanting to be part of expanding public conversations about education and to academics interested in the intersections between media and educational policy.

I argue that understanding rankings requires a form of media education. Often media education is thought of as a subject for children to learn about how advertising is constructed or why some stories make it to the front page and others are ignored, but media education should be more than this. Media are ubiquitous, yet the roles of media in setting the parameters for debates and policies about education, including the role of rankings, are not well understood.

Rankings, with all their flaws, have been extensively documented and studied. But what has not been analyzed is how rankings are part of the larger metaprocess of mediatization (2) through which social, educational, business and political organizations come to organize and communicate through media logics. These logics encompass a belief in commercialization as common sense for public and private spaces. In fact, media and educational institutions have faced similar restructuring: Both media and educational institutions have closed or merged to survive; both get less government support than in earlier eras; both media and educational institutions are perceived as products to be freely traded (for instance, as framed in General Agreement of Trade in Services (GATS)). Deregulation has also allowed for more and larger mergers in both sectors (3, 4).

The mediatization of Higher Education Institutions (HEIs) is happening concurrently with the growing marketization and globalization of education. Within this context, a good education is tied to the commercialization of teaching and research. In the 1960s, the term "internationalization" brought to mind peaceniks and yippies hanging out on many university campuses; today, Philip Altbach argues, internationalization in higher education is a push that could "lead to homogenizing knowledge worldwide" and will "decrease diversity of themes and methodologies" (5: p. 6). Similarly, writers argue government deregulation of media has resulted in fewer media companies with massive holdings that include print, radio, TV and online outlets (6). For instance, Thomson Reuters provides data and analytics to rankers and also owns the Web of Science citation indexing service used for determining research productivity (a major indicator for ranking) and newswire services to distribute ranking news to thousands of media outlets. As I will demonstrate in Chapter 3, rankers collect free information from universities and then package and sell this information back to universities in the form of various tools for benchmarking and monitoring (7). Throughout the book, I will show how different aspects of higher education are being mined to produce new products and services.

Rankings have become powerful mediators of the meaning of educational quality. Perhaps the most significant reason for this development relates to the intersecting rise of media/technology conglomeration in an era of marketization of education. University rankings are circulated through networks of media including newspaper websites, blogs, software, recruitment companies and proprietary databases for collecting information about publications for research productivity indicators. The Internet enables the rapid flow of capital and information that allows rankings to be exploited by different corporate and social actors to promote market-related ends. This book examines the growing importance and impact of rankings within the wider context of mediatization and its role in the global convergence of higher education policies.

What does it mean to be ranked?

An important question is whether the focus on mediatized rankings is expanding or narrowing debates about knowledge and what is and could be a good and worthwhile education. Studies that focus on the role of media in education are recent and still relatively rare; higher education policy is often studied in relation to the state and industry. In contrast, I argue that policymakers have the "meta-capital" to determine education policy, but they must do so within a highly mediatized context. How does the threat of not measuring up to the outcomes determined by external forces influence the ability of government and university policymakers to create institutions that are sensitive to the context they work within? Are there ways that these leaders could be proactive in the context of mediatized higher education?

For previous studies, I have interviewed journalists and policymakers about the role of media in educational policy. A participant who was a communications director explained to me that the media aren't literally in the room, but they are always present; ideas that would not fly with the media are rarely even voiced. The debate about policy options – implicit or explicit – goes through media lenses: How will media perceive this story? Will the proposed policy seem like common sense? University leaders go through a similar process: If we don't participate in the rankings what will happen? What will prospective students think of us and will they even know about us if we do not have the visibility rankings provide? Mediatization plays an active role in constructing discourses about what stands for a "good", "excellent" and "bad" university; however, other logics are also at play, in particular intersecting market and political logics.

What does it mean to be ranked in the 21st century? Rank and rankings mean different things in different contexts as they have over the centuries. Indeed, the etymology of the word "rank" represents the conflicting definitions of university rankings. Rank is defined as to "put in order, classify" or "a social division, class of persons." In Old English, "ranc" was used to describe someone or something that was "proud, overbearing, showy"; and in Middle English, "rank" referred to something "excessive and unpleasant." The word "rancid" is believed to come from the influence of Middle French. The term "rank folly" came into use in the 16th century, which could be the "source for the verb meaning to reveal another's guilt" (1929, underworld slang) (8). Rank went from something unpleasant to hierarchies visualized through military and school uniforms, using stripes and other accouterments to denote distinction.

One to three percent of universities in the world are deemed to be worthy of appearing in popular, global, predominately media-generated rankings (7). Are the 97 to 99% of universities that are not ranked composed of low-class people or are they harassed and abused by overbearing, rancid institutions? We do not know. We do know, however, that the highest-ranking institutions – determined by the media – are richer, whiter, English speaking, and concentrated in Western Europe and North America. We also know that many HEIs compete much more vigorously than ever before for public and private funds to sustain themselves or grow, and that acquiring a high ranking is a coveted asset in this endeavor. And we know media companies own the majority of popular ranking systems, but that universities and governments also create rankings.

What is mediatization?

Rankings operate in mediatized contexts in which media act as "moulding forces" (9) Through the process of mediatization educational and political institutions come to employ "media logics" (10) that include media norms and practices such as writing or speaking in sound bytes and pitching stories that fit within media framing of issues. Universities often use media logics to "brand" themselves, affecting, for example, what they pitch as important research to media, and what they display on their websites. In that sense, how university websites represent their status and prestige, and represent others, including the publics they serve, raises questions about how they situate themselves in relation to ranking.

Mediatization is a contextual process that occurs within material conditions of politics and economics. It is part and parcel of how universities brand themselves in hopes of improving their rankings, but how they do this differs based on geopolitics, and national and local branding, as I will explain in the rest of this book. A relatively miniscule number of faculty and students work and study at ranked universities, yet rankings are widely read and used by policymakers, faculty, students and university administrators around the world. To name but a few countries, China, India, Russia, Germany, France, Malaysia, and Korea have programs and policies aimed at developing at least one world-class university (11).

HEIs have an ambivalent attitude towards rankings. Many universities argue they don't need rankings, yet at the same time many universities spend inordinate time and money to participate in rankings and very few universities opt out of rankings entirely. Universities are caught in a catch-22 of sorts, in which major policy dilemmas arise: If universities do participate in HEI rankings, they are reinforcing a system based in intersecting media, commercial and political logics and practices that have little to do with academic norms of research and inquiry; if they do not participate they risk losing public funding, students and donors in an increasingly competitive and globalized environment. Some universities have tried to push back on rankings by attempting to foster their own public image. Important questions arise at these junctures, including: Do universities have the power to navigate the mediatized context of ranking and educational policymaking? With the increased importance granted to ranking, how have positions of the same universities changed over the years?

There are many rankings that focus on everything from the fame and fortune of a university, to student-teacher ratio, internships, extracurricular activities, school spirit, undergraduate education, employment after graduation, and affordability. There seems to be a ranking to suit each institution. For some rankings, universities are selected by the rankers; for some, universities need to apply to be considered; and for others, universities pay a fee to get one or more stars. Other rankers require universities to spend substantial hours collecting and organizing information in the format required by the ranker. In these circumstances, how universities maneuver among media reports, public demands and policy requirements creates a terrain for a fruitful analysis of higher education's predicament. More particularly, how HEIs engage the mediatization of university rankings provides a conceptual framework for analyzing the growing marketization of education.

Book overview

This book has three parts. I start by providing a framework for understanding rankings and the way they operate in mediatized contexts. Chapter 1 provides a conceptual framework for understanding the nexus between mediatization, university rankings and the marketization of higher education; this chapter also explores the impact of rankings on universities and students in relation to university missions and how universities manipulate rankings. Chapter 2 examines branding in relation to the logic of university rankings. Branding is a tricky business for universities: For example, they must situate themselves among global brands and services, but they also attempt to position the local as attractive and different.

Chapters 3–6 build on the preceding chapters by offering empirical analyses on the interplay between rankings and mediatization. Each chapter offers a snapshot into interconnections between ranking, mediatization and higher education. Chapter 3 investigates how the websites of major ranking sources represent excellence and the economic interests at stake. I focus on what are often referred to as the "Big Three" international rankings: The Academic Ranking of World Universities (ARWU), also known as the Shanghai Rankings, began in 2003; the *Times Higher Education* and Quacquarelli Symonds joined forces in 2004 to create a joint ranking, but in 2009 the two broke up, which resulted in The Times Higher Education World University Ranking (THEWUR) and the QS Ranking. These rankings are arguably the most prominent in relation to resource allocation whether through government or industry dollars or the ability to be highly selective in which students to admit (12). I will examine the products that ARWU, QS and TES Global Ltd offer to higher education institutions. Chapter 4 examines the semiotics of rankings using THEWUR as a case study. THEWUR engage a semiotics of objectivity through colorful tables and graphs that symbolize tradition, capital accumulation and responsible individual choice. In Chapter 5, websites of top-ranked institutions in Canada, China, India, South Africa, the UK and the US are analyzed; I consider how universities are representing themselves and their view of excellence in relation to rankings. There is a growing body of literature that examines the importance of universities from the perspective of branding, but much less research that critically examines websites as field sites. I will detail continuities in sites that are nation-specific and argue that we are witnessing the emergence of a global visual language (13). Chapter 6 will look at how public affairs offices use different rankings including lifestyle, livability, and higher education to recruit students, particularly international students. I draw on empirical findings gleaned from interviewing senior university public affairs/communications staff and analyze them as boundary workers.

The third part of the book includes the conclusion in which I argue that popular rankings are currently driven by corporations and are rife with conflicts of interest. I contend that rankings are an understudied economic sector and that more analysis of the cost of rankings is needed. Finally, I claim that the problem with rankings is they make universities much less responsible to diverse communities and, in fact, discourage what Verna Kirkness and Ray Barnhardt refer to as the "4Rs": respectful, responsible, reciprocal and relevant relationships (14) with diverse communities and the Indigenous territories that provide the space for many universities to exist. Universities need to expand – not constrict – ways of knowing and sharing knowledge. Here I will look to ways of creating spaces for different types of imaginings of what good and worthwhile post-secondary education could be.

1
The Spectacle of Global Rankings

Becoming an economic, ranked citizen

I was talking to some colleagues about young teens I knew who were anxious about getting into the right high school, which required an application process that necessitated more effort than I needed to get into a highly ranked doctoral program! I learned that for many children, this anxiety starts much younger than the teens. I was told about a film called *Getting in … Kindergarten* that would explain it all to me: "Everyone is freaking out. It is a competition like no other. The contestants are four- and five-year-olds, their coaches obsessed New York parents. The goal – a spot at a good kindergarten" (15). The film provides stories of children attending one command "playdate" performance after another in what appears to be an endless quest for a spot in a "top" preschool. This endless quest shows how media-based educational rankings impact parental decisions before children know why their parents are suddenly concerned about their ability to draw a horse or put a peg in the right hole. Clearly media-created rankings will be part of many daily decisions that impact the choices made for them and by them. Arguably, children are socialized into this life of the spectacle so early that by the time children and their parents are looking at post-secondary options, it appears mere common sense to use rankings as a guide to decision-making. Children are also sorted into those families who make good choices for them and those who make bad choices. Absent is discussion of who has the resources to make choices and who does not. The spectacle is that everyone has choice.

Guy Debord famously declared that the "spectacle is not a collection of images, but a social relation among people mediated by images" (16). The spectacle is focused on appearance. The spectacle of ranking conveys dramatic hope and fear. To be ranked highly is to be exceptional, and to not be ranked is to be a nobody in a society where spectacle – high visibility – is essential to be seen as having a worthy existence. To aspire to be highly ranked as an individual or institution requires a form of political labor: Children and adults must show they can make decisions, and making good decisions requires an understanding of relations of power. As the teens I have worked with explained to me, "the essay that shows I'm well rounded and doing stuff my peers do not do" is essential to getting into a top university. Standing out requires knowledge of relations of power. It is a form of political labor that is represented as personal – children and adults making good decisions.

Rankings are a performance in the field of higher education as well. How well institutions perform every year may be looked at as part of a larger spectacle of performance that determine excellence. For Van Parijs, rankings are akin to "being under the spell" of a mystifying dance: "... many universities have been jumping happily up and sadly down, sometimes quite spectacularly, from one year to the next, without this having anything whatever to do with any improvement or deterioration of their real-life performance" (17).

An HEI can be ranked higher or lower compared to other institutions without anything being different in the actual work of the institution or its performance (18). For instance, King Abdulaziz University shot up in the THEWUR and the ARWU rankings by offering lucrative contracts to over 100 foreign academics with strong publication records in the sciences for listing KAU as a secondary affiliation on all of their publications (19). Another example of an increase in ranking was caused by a changing methodology. Some rankers used per pupil expenditure as a proxy of quality, which sometimes has resulted in university leaders including water, library services and electricity as part of what they counted for per student expenditure (20).

Universities have not acquiesced to ranking merely for prestige but to gain international students, which are a key indicator for the "Big Three" (QS, THEWUR and ARWU) in determining whether an institution is world class (21). Some HEIs have merged in hopes that combining resources will improve their ranking. Larger institutions mean more citations, more students, more Science, Technology, Engineering and Mathematics (STEM), and so a better chance at a higher ranking. The impact of rankings on policy varies: "The explicitly expressed motive behind this 'big is beautiful' reasoning is the urge to trim Finnish universities so that they can climb higher in the ladders of the international ranking lists of the world's top universities" (22: pp. 289–290).

In an interview with *Inside Higher Education*, Ellen Hazelkorn, a prolific researcher on the subject of ranking, sums up why we should be concerned about decisions based on university rankings:

> At the end of the day you can say they're a commercial company; they're a business. You want to eat McDonalds all day, we're not telling you it's the healthiest food but it's your choice. But the problem is we have policy makers and others making serious decisions about higher education, about resource allocation and related issues, based on rankings (23).

Hazelkorn's point about choice is central to this book. Rankings are not only used by individuals, but also by media and policymakers to frame winners and losers in the HE landscape. Moreover, rankings influence resource allocation decisions at the government level and the ability of HEIs to recruit students. Some studies maintain institutions are reinventing themselves to focus on research even if the institution historically was recognized for excellence in teaching and service. One study interviewed over 100 law faculty and administrators in the USA (20) to assess the impact of the *US News and World Ranking Report* on them. The authors found that rankings influenced admissions processes and students' decision processes, creating differences through "the magnification of the small and statistically random, distinctions produced by the measurement apparatus" (20: p. 105).

A *New York Times* article aptly titled "Promiscuous College Come-ons" (24) provides examples of how HEIs encourage students to apply. It claims that HEIs "buy data to identify persuadable applicants and then approach them with come-ons as breathless as any telemarketer's pitch." Colleges, for example, send out VIP application letters to get numbers up so that they can reject more and increase their ranking on the all-important selectivity indicator (24). An analysis of *U.S. News and World Report College Rankings* found institutions that appear ranked on the front page of the ranking publication "experience a substantial improvement in admission indicators" (25: p. 432). In other words, universities that are highly ranked receive more applicants and can be more selective, which is helpful for future rankings. Perhaps the most apt and blunt response to the impact of rankings on the behavior of some universities came from Catherine Watt, a former institutional researcher at Clemson University, when asked about the ethics of deliberately manipulating ranking data:

We have been criticized for not fulfilling the mission of a public land-grant institution, Watt responded. But we have gotten really good press. We have walked the fine line between illegal, unethical, and really interesting (26).

Watt was swiftly criticized for her statements by a public affairs spokesperson from Clemson, but substantive evidence was not provided to refute her statement of data manipulation.

The role of public affairs staff as boundary workers who are expected to mediate between the academic and the media world will be elaborated upon in Chapter 6. Data manipulation is well known around rankings; however, a public relations official openly speaking about it is quite rare. These examples are illustrative of a "spectacular economy of education" (27: pp. 339–340). The branding or spectacular show of educational excellence can become more important than actually achieving excellence. Rankings, whether of universities or cities, are a powerful way to manufacture competition across entities or institutions that were previously not in competition with each other (28). As we will see, rankings also create publics or groups.

Adapting/acquiescing to media logics

The ranking process is one about which many HE leaders express ambivalence, while at the same time spending inordinate amounts of time and money to participate. However, there have been moments of resistance to rankings: The then-president of the University of Alberta, Indira Samarasekera, led a boycott in 2007 against the popular *Maclean's* magazine, in which 25 out of over 90 institutions in Canada participated. Samarasekera stated: "It's time to question these third-party rankings that are actually marketing driven, designed to sell particular issues of a publication with repurposing of their content into even higher sales volume special editions with year-long shelf life" (29). In the USA in 2007 the Annapolis Group, consisting of 125 predominately liberal arts colleges, asked members to refuse to fill out the *U.S. News and World Report* reputational survey or use the rankings in any promotional materials (30, 31). In 1999, 35 Asian universities refused to participate in *Asiaweek* (32), and in 2001 *Asiaweek* announced it would no longer produce the ranking (33). The resistance was short-lived, however; government funding cuts after 2008 in many jurisdictions has led to increased pressure to compete for funding.

After 2008, universities appeared in large part to acquiesce to the necessity of rankings and began to focus more on being ranked as "world class." University administrators seem to agree that the rankings are flawed. Rankings presuppose a singular notion of education and that there is only one type of excellent, world-class university. A university's ranking might improve if it channels efforts in this particular direction; however, such a shift should not be conflated with an actual improvement in education. Many rankers assume, for example, that money and class size are directly correlated to quality of education, yet numerous studies show this correlation is simplistic (34). Despite the methodological and epistemological flaws of popular rankings, they are hard to resist. In reference to the *U.S. News and World Report* rankings, Dean of Stanford Law, Larry Kramer, stated: "You distort your policies to preserve your ranking, that's the problem. These rankings are corrosive to the actual education because this poll takes... 12 criteria and now you have to fetishize them" (35). Kramer points to the conflicted reality experienced by university leaders: They know rankings are simplistic, flawed, and corrosive, but refusing to participate can lead to a loss of social and economic capital. Rankings have come to play a role in determining which universities are granted distinction, and universities with the resources to be constantly visible through the use of media logics are more likely to excel in the ranking game. Of course successful deployment of media logics does not in and of itself lead a university to be ranked as world class, as is clear from institutions such as the University of Phoenix; however, top-ranked universities do engage with media logics as part of the overall strategy to be visible – a prerequisite to "world-class" status.

Corporatization and technologies of visibility

Rankings could be approached as a technology of visibility in that through their deployment emphasis is placed on which institutions have exposure and which do not. As technologies of visibility, rankings are therefore implicated in shaping the landscape of HE. Andrea Brighenti advises that visibility is usually asymmetrical:

> When a transformation in reciprocal visibilities occurs, i.e., when something becomes more visible or less visible than before, we should ask ourselves who is acting on and reacting to the properties of the field, and which specific relationships are being shaped. The field of visibility is distinct from all singular visibility flows. It is endowed with its own thresholds of relevance and its multiple ensembles of cones (36: p. 326).

Technology can make it appear that anyone can direct the flow of visibility, or that what is visible is what is popular. Hidden from view are the human decisions that go into how search engines work and how these decisions reshape how and what information is collected and given legitimacy. Technological developments in the last 15 years have changed how rankings render visible or obscure the location of different universities on the HE landscape. The rapid growth of rankings is parallel to the dramatic increase in the ability of technology to turn out massive amounts of what is often referred to as "big data." Boyd and Crawford explain that big data is not merely about lots of data, but the changes in technology that allow the "capacity to search, aggregate, and cross-reference large data sets" (37: p. 665); central to the reverence of big data is a belief in its neutrality and objectivity. Yet, like any data, humans determine what to collect, how to "clean" data, and how to interpret and share it. The Web of Science (WOS), for example, is an influential citation index used by rankers to collect information for research productivity indicators, through a process that has become "conceived as 'universal'" (37: p. 617). Not surprisingly, WOS was created in academic centers that reached the top of the system they themselves created (38). Many regional and national rankings existed before the widespread use of the Internet; however, the proliferation of international rankings is in part due to the increasing representation of "big data" as a neutral decision-maker.

Algorithms, Latzer et al. argue, influence education and other areas of life through automating "nothing less than the commercialization of reality mining and reality construction in information societies" (39: p. 3). This process, the authors argue, is influencing all areas of life. In journalism, an editor looking at various events and news releases in the past would determine what she sees as most newsworthy; however, this type of judgment is replaced by "selection of news in which programmed command lines supplement – if not substitute – the selection of front-page editors, automatically prioritizing news stories" (40: p. 149). The argument could be made for a similar process of mediatization and automation in determining research productivity and excellence.

Closed clubs: a typology of visibility

Institutions with high reputational ranks continue to be ranked highly, with little room for institutions outside of the club to move in regardless of the quality of faculty, students and programs offered. The halo effect is protective for institutions who might not deliver all they state, but members will not publicly state so because association with the brand in and of itself is a powerful form of symbolic and often economic capital. The halo effect is a well-known phenomenon; in one study, for example, university students were asked to listen to a lecturer. The students who were told the lecturer was from a prestigious university and a well-known academic rated him higher and assumed he was 6 centimeters taller than did students who listened to the same lecturer but were told he was low status and from a second-rate university! (41) Simon Marginson argues that a halo effect can also be at play in how universities are perceived. If a university is well known, it is likely to get better reviews regardless of what is actually occurring at the institution (42).

Paradeise and Thoening (21) offer a typology of 4 groups of HEIs in terms of how they respond to rankings: top-of-the-pile universities, the wannabes, the venerables, and the missionaries. The top-of-the-pile groups rely on their massive capital – social and economic – and the order for the top-of-the-pile groups changes very little. The same universities appear in the top 10; Harvard might be 1st one year and 2nd the next, but large changes are unlikely. The wannabes are unlikely to upset a university in the top-of-the-pile, but they ardently hope to do so: "As compared with the agile elephants that top universities are, wannabes may look more like fragile gazelles. The faster they run to reach the top, the less they may build up a sustainable instrumentation" (p. 24).

These universities may have been focused on teaching or service, but to go up in the ranking requires putting these goals aside or at least lessening them to beef up research productivity (i.e. peer-reviewed journal articles counted in databases used by rankers). Wannabes and venerable institutions both have reputational capital, but venerable institutions abhor the external excellence criteria that wannabes jump to fulfill; venerable institutions have history and capital that allows them to appear to dismiss rankings. The missionary HEIs who work with disadvantaged students have clear teaching and service agendas; their concern for access and equity leads them to oppose the imposition of external standards that constrain opportunities for students already disadvantaged. They may try to ignore rankings but often see a decrease in their funding in consequence.

The typology is obviously simplistic but demonstrates how not all institutions respond in the same way to rankings, though all are impacted because of the importance funders – in particular, governments – place on rankings. A glass ceiling, for example, is created that results in high-ranking institutions only talking and recruiting from others in their club (43). African university leaders, for example, spoke to Hazelkorn about the difficulty finding collaborators to work with from high-ranked institutions because the collaboration would not assist their ranking (43). These dynamics suggest rankings reinforce and in some cases create clubs; universities may not have thought of themselves as related, but become linked by their placement on ranking tables. Through this process, new publics can be formed – Caltech may not have been known worldwide 20 years ago, but now it ranks up with Harvard and Oxford and has become a member of the same elite club.

Rankings are a key part of marketing strategies, but it is a risky game. Guelph University in Canada, for example, had all its materials branded when it was ranked #1 in the comprehensive category used by the *Maclean's* magazine ranking, but the following year Guelph went down in the tables and had to rebrand (44).

University rankings as index of economic strength

Higher education has been reshaped as a global commodity that can be used to judge the economic health of nations. Indeed, universities that seek to borrow funds are evaluated by investor companies such as Standard & Poor's and Moody's, and HEIs with high rankings can obtain lower interest rates (45). For popular ranking systems, substantial weighting is given to the percentage of international students and faculty; international students become constructed not as mere students but as a central export needed for the national interest.

International student enrollment is also impacted by rankings; for example, Qatar will only provide scholarships to students going to highly ranked universities (32). A survey found that 77% of HEI policymakers in Europe used rankings in policymaking and setting institutional goals, and a survey of Japanese universities found that 50% of universities used rankings for policymaking and institutional decision-making (43). The ranking of universities, marketers argue, is not just a concern for university leaders, but for policymakers, and industry, as well:

> Considering higher education (HE) is Australia's third largest export, safeguarding the sector against potential new entrants becomes a matter of national interest. ... Forty percent of these 25- to 34-year-olds will be from China and India, which represent Australia's growth markets (46).

Australia has been a leader in ranking as part of branding. The more Australia branded, the more international students came to Australia and with this came an increased ranking for Australia's universities. "Brand Australia," a federal government initiative, was a leader in branding its higher education system. Public funding has decreased in Australia, and subsequently its higher education system has come to rely on international students; ironically, Australian HEIs must compete much more vigorously for them as other players are set on usurping Brand Australia.

Indeed, competition for high ranking is not only a competition between institutions but between nations. Increasingly, governments tie the higher education sector to policies for global economic competitiveness (47). Australia deployed an aggressive media recruitment strategy, but soon other nations got into the game, such as Canada, which created its own Brand Canada marketing campaign; Moody's Investor Service wrote a report stating, "New Canadian immigration policies aimed at increasing international student enrollment that came into effect on June 1, 2014 will enhance the competitiveness of Canadian universities" (48: p. 1).

The focus on rankings can mean countries with few resources spend them in an attempt to get a university into the world rankings, but this may be done at the cost of equity and access (32). Acquiring research stars is a key strategy for increasing reputational rankings: Having a Nobel Prize winner or Field Medal winner on faculty has a direct impact on the ARWU ranking. An academic star can negotiate attractive packages in an internationally competitive marketplace, and garner media attention sought by universities as a strategy for increasing reputational rankings and increasing student application numbers.

Roger King writes: "…under the influence of global university rankings, can be detected widespread governmental ambitions to develop domestic entities as 'world-class universities'…National research and strategic investment policies also appear eerily similar" (49: p. 586). The result is a standardized list of what is considered to be research and education worthy of state support. Governments, universities and professors in their classrooms negotiate dominant trends in different ways, as I will demonstrate in the coming chapters.

Rankings and constructing empires and spheres of influence

University rankings interconnect with other rankings such as *Asiaweek,* the *Economist,* or *Anholt City Brands Index,* which rank cities (28). Governments are aligning higher education, immigration and innovation policies; countries including Holland and Denmark provide preference to prospective immigrants who graduate from top-ranked universities. These meta-processes can be seen as homogenizing forces; however, how different universities and countries experience rankings and how they are mediatized is based in particular historical, political and economic contexts. In the UK, for example, the government marketed the UK as a great place for international students, but the government was blamed subsequently for a decline in international students. Critics argued that the government bringing forward anti-immigration policies left international students feeling unwelcome and looking for other places to study (50).

University ranking schemes are part of an emerging "global meta-policy consensus" (51: p. 461) that operates as both soft and hard power. The aspiration to be a student or faculty member in a world-class HEI serves as a form of soft power. The desire on the part of governments for world-class economic and social capital can lead to the use of hard power, including an HEI gaining or losing funding based on ranking (51). University rankings are, as Lo maintains, "national projects entrenched in the geopolitics of knowledge, and as a technology used by individual countries to achieve their national goals for higher education" (52: p. 63).

Work by a number of scholars points to the increasing pressure Asian scholars are under to publish in English; indeed, academics are not only pressured to publish in English journals, but in journals that are captured by databases used by rankers (53, 54, 55). The result is that academic writing is less about issues of local and national concern (51, 53) and money moves to the richest institutions and away from those that serve the majority of students (17). Because world-class knowledge is seen as English, the hegemony of Anglo-American scholarship is reinforced (56). Özbilgin, in an analysis of editorial boards in his field of human resources management, found that the majority of the editorial boards for journals claiming to be international were composed of white men from North America and Britain. He provides a succinct argument for how this impacts knowledge.

> It would indeed be naïve to locate journal ranking as an objective system outside the subjective relations of power which pervade the academic field. This issue leads me to my second point: Academic labor processes are characterized by multiple inequalities. White men from middle and upper class backgrounds and with other arbitrary entitlements, attributes, and symbols of status dominate elite institutions of research. By virtue of their position, they are the dominant groups in prestigious journals as editors (56: p. 114).

Rankings create boundaries of where students and faculty can go. A student who does doctoral work at a low-ranked institution is unlikely to get a job at a high-ranked institution. The system of ranking does not allow more than a specific number of institutions to be considered world class (57). Furthermore, reputation surveys overwhelming survey European and North American academics who are more likely to know more about universities in North America and Europe than in Asia and Africa.

Conclusion

Rankings are pervasive and both reinforce and create new politics that determine who can move where. The central argument in this book is that rankings need to be seen within the larger context of mediatization of education and the importance accorded to education as an economic driver of nations. As we have seen in this chapter, rankings play different roles at both the level of institutions and at the level of the geopolitics of nations.

2
Seeing Is Believing: University Websites

Before I completed my doctorate in 2002, I attended four post-secondary institutions, only two of which are highly ranked. Nonetheless, I got an excellent education in all four schools I attended. When I attended, not a single one of them had a coherent brand or swag for students beyond a pen and maybe a mouse pad. For sure, there are examples of universities marketing themselves as far back as the 1700s and crests and university colors were commonplace. Thus, marketing universities is not, in itself, new, but the disciplined focus on a coherent brand is. Public affairs offices began to pop up in some universities in the early decades of the 20th century, and the rise of PR and PR professionals sped up in the 1970s and is still climbing in importance (58).

Public affairs offices of the past may have been responsible for news releases about new presidents and for assisting academics who wanted to tell stories about important research findings; the office might also have helped with writing annual reports. However, with a decline in public funding, public relations has become more focused on marketing – and central to marketing is the process of branding a university. Branding in Old English means to burn, and dating from the mid-17th century it came to mean "a mark of ownership made by branding," even of people; starting in 1827, the word began to be used to refer to products. Like the word "rank," there is an evolution in the connotation of this word from negative to positive. University leaders are told by marketing experts to improve "brand experience," "brand awareness," "brand attachment," and "brand architecture." In short, they aim to present a coherent visual identity and to assess the benefits through tracking the brand (59).

The brand is not only the emblem of the university, but the deployment of metaphor. A student jumping in the air can be used to metaphorically represent happiness, success and accessibility and, as we will see in Chapter 5, sometimes linguistic co-text is not needed to get across the message of the branding materials (60). Most universities use terms and images to denote resources and to make their universities seem more accessible, but they also use terms such as "world-class," the "best," or "leading" – a trend that Bélanger contends started with the *U.S. News and World Report* national ranking of universities in 1981 (61). Today, Higher Education (HE) products are big business, with some universities creating companies on stock exchanges (62) and other universities themselves being listed on the stock exchange.

Branding increasingly targets younger populations. Universities now market to younger teens and parents to build "brand awareness" (63). In the first half of 2013, US colleges and universities spent $570.5 million in paid advertising. In the UK, universities have increased the cost of marketing to students to 36 million GBP (64).[1]

There has been a massive rise in spending on marketing in the last four years, coinciding with government cuts and changes in rules that allow universities to take more students. Universities in Australia are leaders in branding: In 2012, Deakin – a top spender there – spent over $14 million on marketing (65). Performing the branding spectacle, which calls for presenting unifying goals, is not only expensive, it requires exclusion and marginalization of some groups. As the general secretary of the university workers union opined: "More money seems to be spent on selling the idea of an education than delivering it. Students are being forced to pay more and staff are not paid enough, yet the marketing budget seems to be unaffected" (66).

Branding is about gaining and maintaining product loyalty. The institution might not deliver all it promises, but members will not publicly admit this because association with the brand in and of itself is a powerful form of symbolic and frequently economic capital. In other words, the product's brand becomes part of an individual's brand. Saying one graduated from a top university carries status and protecting that status becomes paramount.

Consider the recent scandal at Pennsylvania State University. A football coach named Jerry Sandusky was found to be guilty of child abuse over a number of years; it turned out his superiors knew about the abuse for over ten years and did nothing. When the abuse hit the papers, the reported response by the alumni group was largely anger that the brand of their school had been damaged. The head of the alumni organization was quoted in *The New York Times* as being upset that the university settled with the families of victims because this "reinforced perceptions of Penn State's guilt" (67). In this case, reputation becomes a self-reinforcing story that is fiercely protected regardless of harm. The loss of reputation indeed came at a huge cost to Penn State: State Farm pulled ads from Penn State football games (68) and Moody's Investor Services downgraded Penn State from an Aa1 to an Aa2 ranking (69).

Brand management, university leaders are told by higher education marketing journals and the army of new higher education brand professionals, is essential to institutional growth and rankings. Thus, universities are not just looking for students to enroll, but for lifelong customers. Loyal customers come back for further education, send their children to the same institution, and donate money. University websites, marketers advise, should come under brand policies that dictate the look and feel of websites, the size of images, logo use and strategies for dealing with risks to the brand. David Copping, a lawyer writing for the *Times Higher Education*, provides this advice to universities: "Appointing brand guardians and having a proper media management strategy can reduce the risk of brand damage arising from problems with internal core activities" (70). Not surprisingly, then, brand guardians are growing in numbers and job titles. A look at *HigherEdJobs* in April 2015, under the Public Relations, Marketing and Communications section, yielded 546 positions in the U.S. Postings including social media specialists, student recruitment marketers, marketing and community managers, marketing and alumni managers, external relations specialists, news directors, graphic designers, and creative directors. I argue that these professionals are a kind of "boundary worker," tasked with creating permeability between sectors that were previously separated by different norms – and sometimes great animosity. Getting "buy in" and, ultimately, compliance to brand strategy is the job of these boundary workers (71, 72).

Boundary workers

Prior to the 1990s, "marketing was viewed as undignified, even vulgar; university officials thought that students would suffer if recruitment practices went beyond a straight-and-narrow informational approach" (44: p. 567). However, today universities have virtual tours and swag to give away at recruitment fairs, and draws for iPads. University "appointed brand guardians" may come from news media, but also originate from marketing backgrounds in the public and/or private sector. They must walk the boundary between the norms of academics, with their focus on scholarship and academic freedom, and those of university leaders anxious to maintain or increase revenue streams in the face of cutbacks. Increasingly these boundary workers hold senior positions on the leadership teams of universities (73), and they move across boundaries of media, government, education and industry. *The Guardian* in the UK co-sponsored – with a branding consultancy company – a roundtable on university branding in which a participant explained the need for developing

> ...the synergy between marketing and branding; and getting academics on side by linking success in the marketplace to academic freedom. "Even though involving academics is like herding cats, it can be done," said one participant. Without consensus in the university, branding or re-branding can be ineffective (74).

These boundary workers are clear that having academics involved is preferable, but it is akin to entering a house of madness in hopes of bringing light and rationality to the misguided. Branding is a process of disciplining the university in a way that shapes the academic ethos. The language of academic freedom remains, but academics are cautioned to do things that the market finds interesting (74).

The university as unitary ranked entity also influences what is considered high-value research and who are considered high-value researchers: The work of determining what is of interest and how to respond cannot be explained without attention to new media. Universities no longer can fully control what is said about them. Social media allows students and alumni to rate their institutions like they do a restaurant or best-selling novel and rankers distribute ranking through multimedia. Technology also allows universities to aggregate data on visitors to their sites, which provides information for segmenting potential markets and micromarketing them. Branding is a process of stamping territory, which reshapes boundaries, and becomes a way of reallocating resources internally.[2]

Visibility is central to all three major ranking systems. Branding – at research intensive universities – requires reshaping of the work of academics: The more their scholars are cited, the higher an institution's score on research productivity. Sending links to one's articles via Twitter, academic.edu, Research Gate, and individual faculty webpages increases the chance of a document being downloaded and perhaps cited. Constant visibility, marketers advise, also helps with brand recognition and is key to reputation surveys, which are important to being highly ranked. In this process, the distinction between the faculty member as person and producer/consumer becomes blurred.

Nobel Prize winner Randy Schekman argues that obsessing with what he calls "luxury brand" journals is bad for science: "These journals aggressively curate their brands, in ways more conducive to selling subscriptions than to stimulating the most important research" (75). He goes on to compare this to fashion and to creating demand through artificially restricting articles accepted for publication and with a "gimmick" called "impact factor." Pressure to publish flashy studies often leads to "cutting corners: and to retractions of articles" (76). Citation impact factors are often based on the Thomson Reuters Journal Citation Report and the Elsevier SCImago Journal Rank, or, more recently, altmetrics (based on how often a piece of research is cited in YouTube, blogs, tweets, Facebook and news media). Altmetrics like bibliometrics, however, can be gamed; retweets can be purchased.

Promotion through branded partnerships

From rankings, a series of other businesses have emerged, including conference series and branded products to improve rankings. In 2014, the World 100 Reputation leaders and the British Council organized a Reputation Management in Higher Education conference. On its website, The World 100 Reputation Network states it is open to institutions that are in the top 200, for full membership, or other institutions at the associate level based on the "discretion of the committee" (76).

In its latest promotional material, the network includes 46 universities in 17 countries. It is run by the Knowledge Partnership, which provides "independent strategy, marketing and communications consultancy, supporting the education sector with high quality, intelligence-based research." What non-intelligence-based research might be is not clear. Research members pay 5,000 GBP a year for advice on marketing, priority on a world study trip, a webpage profile, and an RSS feed on the network's page. Membership is contingent on not sharing information with non-members. The reader is further told: "The World 100 Reputation Network is a group of the best universities in the world, undertaking research that enhances professional activity in and around reputation management, international relations and strategy" (76). What "professional activity" means is vague, as is the term "international relations." The language of academe, research, inquiry, and education is again absent. The World 100 Reputation Network's language of rankings supplants the language of education and makes a focus on reputation management appear to be simply common sense: "The theme of reputation management has now gained great traction in Japan and beyond, with the aspiration of institutions to feature in the international rankings acting as a powerful motivating force" (77). Here again brand management – not improvement of research or educational opportunities – is the focus. This represents the restructuring of debates within higher education. Talking about academics is complicated, but talking about reputation is easy – it becomes good versus bad. Louise Simpson, director of the World 100 Reputation Network, has developed tools for assessing media that, in turn, are connected in promotional literature to being able to justify budget increases for communication to compete with peers. Brand management is also connected to being better able to show research impact for research assessment exercises and how much impact a university's brand has in relation to competitor universities. Extensive testimonials are provided from PR officials and senior leaders at universities that subscribe to the service, which costs 4,000 GBP a year. Here we see the confluence of products – universities, marketers and media – in the mediatization of higher education policies and politics. But is what we are seeing new or merely part of long-standing efforts to jockey for position in the marketplace of ideas? Are websites in this marketplace akin to the role of medieval art many centuries ago when universities were emerging as institutions for the education of upper-class young men? Universities for centuries have had crests and robes to distinguish what university lineage they herald, or in medieval times

> where saints and mythological or biblical characters were recognized not on the basis of their physiognomy but on the basis of their attributes (Jupiter carrying the thunderbolt, St Catherine carrying the wheel)...the model becomes a construction worker because of an attribute. Take off the hard hat and, with the addition of a drawing board, she could become an architect (13: p. 324).

In some ways, similar to medieval art, branding is predictable – a designer needs to know the rules and apply them to be effective. However, unlike religious art, branding attempts to be universal, and the images are more likely cheerful, with happy and content people rather than images of spiked wheels and violent deaths. An outsider coming into a Catholic church would not necessarily know what was meant by St. Catherine carrying a wheel, or why Jupiter was darting thunderbolts all over the place. If, in medieval times, one was transported from ancient China to England, a woman carrying a wheel might not have meant much. However, Western branding of education is far more pervasive and faster to travel throughout the world than Jupiter or Catherine. David Machin argues that a global visual language is emerging with the advent of the Getty Image bank, which provides millions of generic, high-quality images to industry, government, education and media institutions.

Institutions increasingly rely on these images rather than taking their own, and use the same style of image to denote freedom, contentment and identity with a brand (13). As I will demonstrate in Chapter 5, there appears to be a growing similarity in the type of images used by university websites across national and cultural contexts.

Website politics

Websites are the key location for a university to promote itself to the world. Websites have a basic grammar that is reflected in part by where images are placed and how the hierarchy of links is constructed. A website, like a movie or a book, can be interpreted in different ways, but a producer can – through images, color, sequencing, and place-ment – influence the way a reader moves through the space (78). In this sentence, there is an order to subjects and verbs, adjectives and adverbs. Subjects and verbs tell us about identity and action – who is the subject and what is he/she/it doing? There are, of course, many variations in the order of subject and verbs and use of adjectives and adverbs, based on language used, culture, and the audience the website is intended for, but there is still an order. The grammar of websites also has its own syntax through which viewers make meaning.

Of course, websites, unlike newspapers, do not have a fold, but the terminology is still used to speak about content from most important to least. Above the fold refers to content that does not require scrolling. In other words, what is above the fold is what the producer most wants the reader to see. Websites, then, are a form of politics that tells audiences who and what is important, based on choices of images, placement, sequencing of information and choice of linguistic text.

Branding relies on the cosmopolitan reach of commercial messages. For universities, this presents a dilemma: How does a physically based institution negotiate cultural diversity in the context of branding to the planet? What clear message does one provide? Who decides the univer-sality of these messages? Increasingly, universities hire consultants to help them with these matters; indeed, some universities contract with consultants from ranking organizations or the World 100 Reputation Network to tell them how to improve their strategies for branding as part of a strategy to rise in the rankings. Other universities, as I will detail in Chapter 6, structure and restructure to ensure their internal and external branding is aligned with alumni affairs, development, industry and government relations. The public affairs or boundary workers are the people that implement what these consultants suggest.

To compete in a marketplace where bodies, things and nature are for sale requires the seller to differentiate the product. It means cornering desire – the desire to belong, to have status and to be recognized. The original product or service may not be relevant, but the appearance of having it is key to citizenship based on consumption. Universities that move beyond their original context need to manage multiple images at the same time, but to present a branch campus of a North American university as having the same resources as the home campus presents challenges. Branch campuses have fewer resources and often have difficulty in finding faculty with the same educational and research background as those at the home campuses; however, if the university is high status, the desire to identify with it will most likely quell open criticism. Ironically, for a student to criticize a highly ranked university would be to disrupt his or her own identity as a graduate of that venerated institution. It is also unlikely a prospective employee will say in an interview, "Did you know I am from a top university that lets rich kids get in with low marks, or that I was taught by overworked TAs and that the institution covered up sexual assaults to preserve its reputation?" Similar to the Penn State alumni's protest, honesty has its costs. University website politics are central to forming identities through telling students and faculty who is most important based on who and what is located where.

The intricacies of branding: conveying lifestyle and landscape

Central to branding a lifestyle are websites that provide the visual evocations of a lifestyle. The goal of a branded website is to foster the emotional attachment that results in loyalty to a brand, but this presents challenges: Stores construct an ambience, through selecting music, lighting and employees that embrace and represent their brand; website designers attempt to replicate these sensory stimuli online, but, as Rosen & Purinton argue, "For the e-retailer, the sensory shopping experience must be played out on the template of the web page" (79). Competing for students who have choices among many universities, all claiming to offer the same academic programs, requires differentiating ancillary products such as nice dorms and good food. The language of promotion is shifting the educational discourse from students to consumers with universities as good or bad products. Marketers advise universities to assume that prospective students are making choices not just on academic reputation, but also on whether the sports facilities are top-notch, the dorms are attractive, and the food is appealing. Online visuals of fun and excitement dominate higher education websites and view books (80). Branding a lifestyle or identity becomes central in this context, and this is done through a combination of images, audio and text.

What universities show as their brand depends on their socio-political location. A university that is seen as local or regional will not have the narratives of greatness of a Harvard. They will need to be constantly competing and looking to rebrand to appear distinctive. Conversely, Harvard can "generate income from the associative value of the (copyrighted) school name" (p. 567); they can brand clothes, continuing education, and a host of other products (81).

A website can provide almost limitless information, and a reader can enter and exit in multiple ways. A skillful website designer, however, like a choreographer, focuses the audience's attention carefully: Too much, for example, and the audience loses the plot; too little and the viewers click to the next site. Audience members may attend to different parts of the stage, but the choreographer can also limit distractions in hopes they will attend to a focal point such as a large picture in the middle, or main dancers versus the chorus; indeed, the designer can influence the ways a reader moves through the website by building a hierarchy of links. The human decisions about website construction provide a window for outsiders and insiders to see what is most important to the leadership of the university. Indeed, the choreography of faculty and student bodies becomes part of the performance: The design may appear seamless as if all dancers are playing an equal role, but like any performance, there must be an order and a hierarchy; some dancers are given prominence, even if the appearance is of a utopian collective where all are equal. Promotional websites are designed to provide a sense of intimacy and to deny the presence of hierarchies of consumers and producers.

In a global marketplace with multiple choices, focusing only on what a product does will not distinguish it from others: Thousands of universities provide undergraduate and graduate degrees. To succeed, universities may choose to use the symbolic capital provided to them by ranking – if they want to score highly. A content analysis of websites from eight countries found differences in layout, color schemes and differences in use of link-based versus graphic-based websites (82). Some studies show that US sites focus less on tradition and authority than Indian or Chinese sites, and American sites emphasized current events more than the future. A number of studies have looked at cultural differences in what audiences see as trustworthy.

Studies in Singapore, for example, point to the growing role of branding universities. Ng argues this is particularly prevalent with the growing deregulation of higher education in Singapore (83). He found that SMU, the first private university in Singapore, aggressively marketed itself as dynamic, collaborative and empowering through unrealistic images (e.g., students throwing a dean in the air). The website focus was on feelings rather than content and images included generic backgrounds with smiling students jumping in the air. Other universities tried to emulate SMU, but their photographs became archetypes in front of a corporate landscape rather than actual individuals in a particular location.

Having a powerful brand becomes key for attracting not only students but also "world-class" academics who are often courted by more than one institution. The beauty and cosmopolitanism of a city become recruiting inducements: Universities sell their city along with their university, and rankers such as QS provide students with information on the "10 most beautiful cities for students." Studies point to prospective students being attracted to traditional architecture and quad spaces (84) and university leaders and brand managers are advised to focus on amenities and a lifestyle, not hard work and academics.

Geography has also become an important part of branding; cities themselves are marketed to become lifestyle concepts (85). Xiong found cities in China used similar strategies to attract students and faculty by referencing their unique characteristics with titles such as "Heavenly State" (p. 327) to emphasize beauty. Celebrity, academics and alumni are also mentioned, as is the history of the institution. The images of innovation, community, stability, and a bright future can become more real than the real.

The hyper-real university

It was in this vein that Baudrillard (86) famously announced "The Gulf War did not happen." He was not arguing that atrocities did not occur, but that the Gulf War was a spectacular show of force that was based in the exchange of signs and commodities that visualized a huge threat to America – one which did not exist in fact. The image is more real than the real. To extend this analogy to what is occurring in higher education, the university might be entirely different than the brand, but the brand becomes paramount: The goal of the university becomes to protect the brand.

If the university is a simulacrum, what happens in it becomes irrelevant – the image becomes everything. The faculty and students are not needed – indeed stock photos can be used to represent the university. The University of Wisconsin, for example, Photoshopped Diallo Shabazz, a young Black man, into their recruitment material; he was not a student at the school, and he did not give permission for his image to be used. The Photoshop image, however, created a simulacrum of diversity. Indeed, the less diverse a campus is, the more pictures they are likely to have of racial diversity (87). The Black body is encoded to provide evidence for what does not exist in the physical space of the campus. However, the simulacrum does not completely eclipse thought – students and others caught the Photoshop job and resisted the attempt at what American satirist Stephen Colbert calls "truthiness."[3]

Journals such as the *Journal of Higher Education Marketing* include articles such as "Do professors have customer-based brand equity?" that detail which professors students see as competent and helpful (88). It is not surprising that universities hold branding workshops. Faculty members also become consumers of rankings, of products sold by ranking, and producers of citations and reputation that are used by other producers/consumers, including students, government and industry. But the producers and consumers are not equal: The rankers, not faculty members, determine what is good and worthwhile education, and faculty members, as in other corporate environments, are provided incentives for becoming consumer/producer advocates for their university's brand.

Conclusion

Having multiple ways of knowing and doing research in universities becomes a problem if branding one coherent product becomes the primary institutional goal; the solution to this new problem then becomes narrowing what is seen as legitimately academic, that is, what is educational. This focusing is perhaps best exemplified by the most visible aspect of the hyper-real university: Its website.

The university website is composed of steps. Increasingly, those steps for highly ranked universities are predictable and provide a sense of naturalness and ease: The reader will not see the various stages of market research – focus group testing, analysis of other highly ranked university websites, and Google Analytics[4] – that mask the tensions between understanding the university as a unitary brand and the university as a forum for debating multiple ways of knowing and understanding the world. Indeed, websites fit within larger processes of mediatization, an activity that is affected by not only cultural but also economic policies and contexts, as I will show in the next chapter.

3
Who Is Watching the Watchdogs? The Business of Rankings

When I started as a professor in 2003, I knew very little about rankings, but soon I could not attend a meeting or convocation without being told I was part of an elite club – a top-ranked school, a world-class school. A colleague from another university explained how his dean sent a proud letter when they went up in the rankings; the following year, however, their ranking went down, and my colleague received an email saying not to worry – the rankings were flawed. I started to count references in meetings to rankings or the importance of being "world class". What began as a strategy to pass the time in stuffy rooms ultimately led me to begin to question the power and reach of rankings. Today there are 10 global rankings and over 150 national or specialist rankings (89). How did predominately media-generated rankings become such a ubiquitous marker of success, academic quality and legitimacy?

To answer this question, I will first map the field of the "Big Three" rankings – ARWU, also known as the Shanghai Ranking; the QS; and the Times Higher Education World University Ranking (THEWUR). In the second part of the chapter, I will examine the networks of power that are involved in different rankings, including movement within and across ranking and fields. I am especially interested in looking at the websites of rankers and a ranking regulator (IREG) as examples of mediatization. Mediatization studies have been criticized for focusing on how institutions interact with media and ignoring the complex web of industries that are central to understanding mediatization of social, cultural and political spheres (90). In this chapter, however, I approach higher education as a field with many players including rankers, which, in turn, includes industry, academia, government and media. A number of theorists including Nick Couldry have connected mediatization theories to Pierre Bourdieu's work, particularly around social fields. Bourdieu points to the meta-capital of the state, but Couldry shows that it is not only the state that has meta-capital, but media as well.

> We could hypothesize that the greater the media sector's meta-capital, the more likely the salience of media-related capital for action in any particular field, but this would not be a general logic, but rather an emergent process from transformations under way in many fields simultaneously" (91, p. 9).

In other words, the meta-capital of media interacts with dynamic processes of change within and across fields such as education and industry.

Mediatization involves processes and practices which as Rawolle and Lingard remind us: "act over time to change power relations between people situated in different fields" (92: p. 271). The ways in which individuals cross between the fields of education, media, government and business change as do power relations. Couldry demonstrates that mediatization is useful for understanding "different types of process across different sites," which is compatible with field theory and its insistence on multiple logics (91: p. 6).

Pierre Bourdieu developed conceptual tools to understand how people work within and across what he referred to as fields; within and across these fields there are relations of power that structure action. Bourdieu made an analogy to physical force fields to explain that a social field is a place where people's action creates a reaction; however, they are acting based on permanent dispositions; that is, actions are within parameters that constrain how we act if we wish to be a member of a field. A field is a social space that is relational and historical (93). Within academia, for example, there are faculties, and those faculties are positioned differently; for example, the researcher in engineering who patents her invention may feel closer to the field of business than academia. The existence of the field is based in accepting the logics of practice and what Bourdieu called illusion – the belief that the rules are worthy of obeying and make sense to members.

A field like journalism can interact with other fields such as education, and these relations are not static. All fields exist within spaces of other fields, such as economics; indeed, a field establishes the "rules of the game." For example, a central rule of the academic game is competition: Students are ranked according to others from a young age, and this continues through graduate school and the life of a professor. Mediatized rankings draw on this accepted rule of the game, but translate and subvert it to the meta-capital of media and commercial logics. By going beyond seeing educational policy as negotiated between government and public education stakeholders, we can examine the role of private industries in influencing, creating, and implementing educational policies. We can also better understand the meta-capital of government and media in determining what is represented as a good and worthwhile education.

Table 3.1 provides the indicators used by ARWU, QS, and THEWUR to determine what counts as a world-class higher education institution. The information was drawn from information located on the three rankers' websites in January 2015.

Table 3.1   Indicators used by the "Big Three"

Rankings	ARWU	QS	THEWUR
Quality of education	Measured by # of alumni who have won Fields Medals or Nobel Prizes **10%**	Faculty-Student Ratio **20%**	Teaching (the learning environment) **30%**
Research output	Papers indexed in SCI or SSCI **20%** Highly cited researchers **20%**	Citation per faculty in Scopus database **20%**	Citations (research influence) **30%**
Prizes	Faculty won Fields and Nobel Prizes **20%** and papers published in Science of Nature **20%**		
Reputation		Academic survey **40%** Employer survey **10%**	Research volume (income and reputation) **30%**
Industry			Income from industry **2.5%**
International		International students **5%** International faculty **5%**	International outlook **7.5%**
Per capital performance	Weighted scores across five indicators divided by FTE academic staff **10%**(94)		

Hazelkorn demonstrates that most of these indicators "measure research or research related activity; this equates to 100% in ARWU, 85% in THE, and 70% in QS" (95: p. 23). I will now analyze each of the three rankings in turn and what the indicators tell us about assumptions of what a world-class university is and should be.

The Big Three

The academic ranking of world universities (ARWU)

Rankings, as discussed in Chapter 1, are not new; however, a university ranking scheme purporting to be international, popularized by media and used by policymakers signaled a new era. The ARWU, also known as the Shanghai Ranking, was created by Shanghai Jiao Tong University in 2003 as part of the government's "985 Project" to encourage Chinese universities to pursue world-class status (96). In an interview in *The Chronicle of Higher Education* in 2008, the creator of the ARWU ranking, Dr. Liu, explained that the university was concerned it was sliding from "its prerevolution position as one of China's premier universities," and that he was tasked with being the "university's inaugural director of strategic planning" (96). As part of his role, he developed the ranking, which was set up for Chinese use only; however, it soon reached international audiences.

The Chinese government saw the ranking as useful for improving the competiveness of Chinese universities (96). The ARWU came at a time when China was growing as an international economic and political player and reflected the government's desire for universities to compete with the outside world. The ARWU rankings were, in consequence, based on Euro-American-centric data, including ascertaining a university's research strength based on publications in English, numbers of Fields Medal and Nobel Prize winners among faculty or alumni, and publications in *Science* and *Nature*. ARWU indicators have been criticized for favoring STEM[1] areas and further marginalizing the social sciences and humanities; beginning in 2013, publications from the SSCI (Social Sciences Citation Index) were added. Another source of criticism is the Highly Cited Researchers list as determined by Thomson Reuters. Especially problematic was the revelation that universities in Saudi Arabia were paying highly cited researchers, mainly from USA universities, to list them as a secondary affiliation, thereby boosting the ranking of Saudi universities (97).

ARWU continues to be critiqued for, on one hand, claiming that it is impartial and that it uses independent data and, on the other hand, relying on Thomson Reuters indexes. Additionally, it is challenged for its focus on English publications, simplistic use of bibliometrics, and not taking into account the size of the university in determining its productivity (98). Some criticisms are debatable. ARWU was critiqued for incompetent analysis of data from Thomson Reuters (99) and of creating results (100) that were not reproducible; however, other academics have argued that the results are indeed reproducible and useful because they are based on the hard evidence of research productivity numbers (98). Of course, determining productivity based on branded journals, particularly in science and technology and only in English, is a highly political and subjective decision.

When I began analyzing ranking websites in 2011, the ARWU homepage was text based and informational; however, in 2015, the homepage uses more images and promotional text. There are rotating images with high production values, including "Ranking of Top Universities in Greater China – 2014" (101). To the side is a series of tables that display little national flags and a listing of top universities, and readers are told that since 2003 the ARWU has been "based on transparent methodology and reliable data. It has been recognized as the precursor of global university rankings and the most trustworthy one" (101). Readers are further assured that, "The Center for World-Class Universities (CWCU) of Shanghai Jiao Tong University is dedicated to the theoretical study of world-class universities and policy applications" and that it receives a great deal of attention "from universities, governments and public media all over the world" (101). Under "About us," viewers learn that the rankings are "conducted by researchers at the Center for World-Class Universities of Shanghai Jiao Tong University" (101). ARWU asserts its leadership in the study of world-class universities and its actual ranking is "published and copyrighted by Shanghai Ranking Consultancy." Finally readers are assured that the "Shanghai Ranking Consultancy is a fully independent organization on higher education information and not legally subordinated to any universities or government agencies" (101). ARWU has a Facebook page and Twitter account, but the main audiences appear to be universities and government policymakers. There are no images of students, and products are focused at the institutional level (e.g., benchmarking, conferences aimed at university leaders and staff responsible for branding).

The ARWU started off just ranking, but now it provides other products and consulting services. The Global Research University Profiles homepage consists of rotating images, including a hand with a mobile phone pointing towards the viewer; not surprisingly, the content is the

ARWU rankings. Images of an origami bird also bookend a picture of a tablet, with, again, information about ranking; the movement of the bird and the tablet together signal the exciting mobility that awaits adventurous students. Origami is exotic – but not too exotic. By using a drop-down menu with a number of indicators, readers can estimate an institution's rank and can also use a benchmarking tool to judge performance in relation to other universities.

QS and Times Higher Education

The ARWU was followed in 2004 by a joint ranking owned by Quacquarelli Symonds (QS) and *The Times Higher Education Supplement*. The development of the QS-THES World University Rankings arose soon after the Review of Business-University Collaboration in the UK, which was commissioned by the UK government. Sir Richard Lambert was an editor for the *Financial Times* from 1991 to 2001 and also a member of the momentary policy board for the Bank of England. Lambert's commission focused on moving universities to cultivate more direct links to industry; not surprisingly, one of his recommendations was to "encourage the development of a league table of the world's best research-intensive universities" (102: p. 126). One benefit of the suggested league tables – also known as rankings – would be to allow government to support entrepreneurial market research. Lambert did not suggest universities create rankings, but that they should encourage the private sector to do so. In response, two large companies joined forces in 2004 to create the QS-THES ranking, and Martin Ince, who had been a deputy director of THE, was hired to manage the new entity.

QS-THES

The joint ranking ran from 2004–2009. QS was responsible for collecting data that it entrusted to Evidence Ltd, which was founded by an academic, Jonathan Adams, and was bought by Thomson Reuters in 2009. THE had the responsibility for the structure and commentary on the rankings and QS was known at the time for student placement services and recruitment with a focus on MBA programs. Today QS continues to be focused on business:

> QS links high achievers from the graduate, MBA and executive communities around the world with leading business schools, post-graduate departments at universities and with employers, through

websites, events, e-guides and technical solutions.... Our ambition is to be the world's leading media, events and software company in the higher education field (103).

Here we see the crossing of numerous fields – education, technology, and media. *Times Higher Education*, at the time of the joint ranking, was known for its media strength in reporting educational issues and connections to policymakers and educators, particularly in the UK. In 2004, 500 universities were chosen based on research impact and, later, some were added based on the *Asiaweek* rankings (104). Subsequently, changes were made to how citations were counted; for example, in 2007, modifications prevented institutions from voting en masse from their own institution through reputation surveys.

In 2009, *Times Higher Education* split from QS, citing concerns that the QS methodology favored the sciences and that their reputation survey was highly problematic. Forty percent of the ranking was based on an opinion survey that in the end was one of the reasons Phil Baty gave for the separation between QS and THE; indeed, the survey was sharply criticized as biased by a number of academics. Martin Ince stayed with QS and Phil Baty with THE. I will describe the disagreement between QS and THE more in the second part of the chapter, which focuses on the movement of people across and within the ranking field. Although it's difficult to discern what the actual motivations behind this decision are, the result was the emergence of the "Big Three."

QS

Quacquarelli Symonds' (QS) managing director is Nunzio Quacquarelli, a graduate of Wharton business school. QS lists many influential media partners including *The Guardian, 24hrs,* IELTS, British Council, *Times of India* and *The New York Times*. For example, *The Guardian* had a webpage for the "QS world university rankings 2014: top 200" which included a hyperlink for "methodology" that led directly to the QS site and its webpage on methodology. The fusing of media and rankings is naturalized. Questions that might arise from an august media company failing to provide its own analysis of the QS methodology and instead handing the task over to the business itself is made seamless through the process of mediatization.

QS has 6 indicators: 40% based on an academic reputation survey, 10% employer reputation, 20% faculty-staff ratio, 20% citations per faculty from Scopus database, 5% international students and 5% international faculty (105). QS has faced perhaps the most criticism from academics. For example, Elizabeth Redden, in a story for the online news magazine *Inside Higher Education,* relays the story of an untenured professor who does online surveys to make a little money. Usually the surveys were about low-stakes issues like toilet paper, but one day he received the QS World University Ranking. The survey was sent by a company to which QS outsources (23). Simon Marginson is quoted in the article, providing his perspective on QS: "Essentially what they have done is they've got a ranking process which they've done very cheaply because they don't do it very well, and that's a loss leader for a lot of other business activities" (23). Philip Altbach further critiques the International Ranking Expert Group (IREG) for giving QS the IREG audit stamp of approval: "the audit is well-intentioned but 'a little bit like the fox guarding the chickens. It's the rankers doing the accreditation of the rankers'" (23). Redden does state Marginson's ties to THE and ARWU.

When Redden's article was reprinted in the HES, Ben Sowter (Head of the Intelligence Division for QS) attacked the credibility of Marginson, stating he is biased because of his involvement with ARWU and THE. What is interesting is the competing use of cross-field validators. Phil Baty, a journalist, defends two academics – Simon Marginson and Philip Altbach – who are criticized as lacking impartiality given their involvement in other rankings (106). Here we see a battle for symbolic capital: Marginson has the symbolic capital of being an academic expert, but Sowter responds by arguing Marginson is really more competitor ranker than academic. Marginson attacks QS as lacking an understanding of basic research and integrity. Journalist Phil Baty, who expresses outrage that such a well-respected academic would be accused of bias, reinforces the third-party validation of Marginson's academic expertise (107). Kevin Downing, director of knowledge enterprise and analysis at City University of Hong Kong, wrote an article for *University World News,* in which he deploys Philip Altbach's concerns about rankings privileging established institutions, and Downing concludes that QS is the best ranking for new universities "eager to establish their credentials on the global stage" (108).

Online commentary also provides a venue to counter the claims of competitors. In an online comment response to Downing's article Baty implicitly argues that Downing is biased by his involvement in QS. Once again Altbach's name is deployed to argue the superiority of one ranking over another:

I'm surprised that Downing, who is Chair of QS's Middle East and Africa Professional Leaders in Education (MAPLE) academic conference committee, quotes Philip Altbach, but does not include perhaps his most decisive comment on the global university ranking systems he has made. Altbach's recent article, "The Globalisation of College and University Rankings," in *Change* magazine, Jan/Feb 2012, says: "The QS World University Rankings are the most problematical" (108).

Sowter and Baty are employees of their respective rankings and in this capacity act as full-time brand guardians. Neither is an academic researcher and both selectively draw on the work of experts in higher education. Altbach and Marginson are known for their cogent critique of rankings, but the critique is clearly not part of the marketing for THEWUR or QS. The deployment of their names to point to the flaws of one brand is constructed as a validator for the other brand.

QS also claims objectivity and seeks academic validators for media pieces. The "peer review survey" that has been the object of criticism is defended by drawing on the apparent usefulness of political polls. On the QS website, under the heading "Understanding the methodology: QS University Rankings," the reader is told that QS brought in experts to make sure the "survey design could not be gamed" and, furthermore, "the survey design is founded on the principles of many online political polls, which have become increasingly accurate at anticipating election results" (109). While QS's statement ignores literature that points to ongoing challenges with political polls (112), even more interesting is its focus on an apparent technique that cannot be gamed. Expert opinion is further called upon in the form of Sir Richard Sykes, the rector of Imperial College London, who assures readers that "an academic review is an appropriate way to compare universities. It takes smart people to judge smart people" (110). Who determines which smart people are called upon to provide judgment and the beliefs and values behind these judgments is not made explicit.

Products and spin-off products

In the center of the QS World University Ranking webpage is a picture of a fierce-looking lion, ready to catch and destroy his prey, above the caption, "Who Rules? Click here to find out." Education is represented as a deadly competition in which hunter is separated from prey by alma mater. The underlying message is that danger is ever present; but with the help of the QS rankings, you too can learn to be a hunter-ruler in the jungle of contemporary society – particularly if you enroll in a business program (a focus for QS).

One of the most fascinating documents I found begins with an image of an animated brain, framed with the QS logo above and below it – *Intelligence Unit: Trusted, Independent, Global Guide To Services*. The 28-page pamphlet explains:

> The QS Intelligence Unit (QSIU) was formed in 2008 as a distinct and autonomous department in order to meet the increasing public interest for comparative data on universities and organisations, and the growing demand for institutions to develop deeper insight into their competitive environment (110: p. 1).

Listed are universities that make the QS top 100, such as MIT, but many clients are from countries with no QS-ranked universities. For those that don't make top world university status there is, for a fee, the "QS star system": "QS Stars uses a rating system that allows a university to shine irrespective of its size, shape and mission" (110). The QS World University Ranking and the stars appear alongside each other. Universities that choose the star option first pay $9,850 for the QS Stars Audit Fee, which is valid for three years; then they pay an annual license fee of $6,850. Universities can also sign up for benchmarking, and for this they pay $45,000 over three years to be benchmarked against six institutions. To add institutions, there are additional fees. Universities also sign up for reputation services. For the "Basic Peer Package," they pay $55,000 and, not surprisingly, more institutions can be added for more money. Ben Sowter explains to a *New York Times* writer that some institutions are happy with two or three stars: "In a world where Harvard is five stars, why wouldn't you want to be seen as a three-star school?...Plenty of people are happy to stay in three-star hotels" (111). The assumption seems to be that elites will always be elites, and that the average person should be happy to pay for a star or two, and maybe even three, with perhaps a few bedbugs to go along for the ride. Clearly, these products raise a number of ethical questions. Nowhere is it made clear that stardom comes with a steep price tag.

The movement of QS services is international with clients speaking to other clients or prospective clients at conferences such as the QS-Apple ©. Apple does not seem to refer to Apple Inc., but I assume is meant to evoke knowledge. "The conference supports the efforts of Asian universities to internationalise by providing valuable opportunities for networking, exchanging best practices and debating new developments in higher education in this dynamic region" (112). Readers are told that "QS-APPLE has the declared mission of helping to build world-class universities for Asia Pacific communities through global partnership and collaboration" and that they have "Our loyal, blue-chip client base" (112). Listed are a number of universities, including MIT, LSE, Stanford, Wharton, NUS, Melbourne and Hong Kong University. Also noted are "blue chip business partners", which include "over 200 multi-nationals and regional recruiters including Goldman Sachs, Morgan Stanley..." and media partners from North America and Asia. The conferences provide mobility between these sectors in support of not just rankings, but student placement services, language services, media and employer recruiters looking for a highly educated mobile workforce.

In 2013, QS announced a new product, the BRICS rankings, to compare educational institutions in the "newly industrialized" nations of Brazil, Russia, India, China and South Africa:

> The project, developed by QS in collaboration with Russian news agency Interfax, emerged from a desire to better highlight and track progress made by each of the five BRICS countries in the higher education field, and to facilitate comparison of universities in nations that share certain key socio-economic dynamics (113).

QS spin-off products – e.g., QS Best Cities for Students, QS Asia, QS Latin America, QS BRICS, Top under 50 Universities (which is visualized with the image of an adorable little lion cub) – are tailored to new markets and revenue sources. As we will see, the Times Higher Education Ranking also provides a suite of interconnected products.

The Times Higher Education Ranking

The Times Higher Education World University Rankings (THEWUR) are owned by TES Global. The organization's website asserts it has a distinctive place among ranking organizations:

> Across Higher Education, TES Global owns and produces the award-winning Times Higher Education (THE) magazine; The Times Higher Education World University Rankings (WUR), the THE World Summit Series and THE Awards. The WUR are the only global university performance tables to judge world class universities across all of their core missions – teaching, research, knowledge transfer and international outlook. The rankings are trusted by students, academics, university leaders, industry and governments (114).

In this explanation of the rankings, the *Times Higher Education* has become THEWUR, thereby marking territory as the only legitimate World University Ranking. The language of trust is sprinkled throughout the website, yet who these academics and leaders are is unstated, and the reader is left to assume that all individuals that matter in these groups trust and look at WUR for guidance.

TSL Education became TES Global in 2014 and in 2013 was acquired by TPG Capital, one of the largest private equity firms in the world that specializes in real estate, buyouts, acquisitions in health care, media and a plethora of other industries (115). It is understandable why TSL Education is a good investment opportunity – e.g., it is supported largely by teachers uploading their lesson plans and other work and universities freely providing data for THE rankings. The TES homepage tells readers it has 7.7 million registered users, up to 1 million resources downloaded a day, 82 per cent of teaching roles advertised filled in 4 weeks and 800 universities now ranked in the Times Higher Education University Rankings (115). THEWUR has five categories and 13 indicators: 30% teaching (learning environment), 30% on citations (impact), 30% on research (income, reputation, volume), 2.5% on industry income and innovation, and 7.5% on international outlook (includes number of international staff, students and research) (116). They have spin-off rankings, including BRICS & Emerging Economies, 100 Under 50 (universities under 50 years old), Asia University Rankings, and World Reputation Rankings.

Like QS, TES Global also acts as a recruiting agency, but not just for higher education: "TES Global exists to drive up standards of education by putting the right teachers in the right jobs and giving them the tools to be the very best that they can be" (115). The tools include sharemylesson.com and other spaces where teachers upload and download materials (115). It is assumed educational institutions that want to be world class should have the same core mission. A language of tough love and benevolence is used to explain why the BRICS & Emerging Economies Rankings is needed:

> Only five institutions from the emerging economies appear in the World University Rankings 2013–14 top 200 (with 38 in the top 400). Some of the most exciting and dynamic institutions from the developing world do not yet make the grade…. This is where the inaugural BRICS & Emerging Economies Rankings come in. There is growing demand for global league tables that reflect regional and economic contexts, and an increasing range of institutions want to benchmark themselves against the world's best, using the clear definitions developed with our

data partner Thomson Reuters that underpin the tough but trusted standards set by the World University Rankings (117).

Universities are represented as trying, but still remedial. E for effort, but they still "do not yet make the grade"; however, with the help of the TR standards that are "tough" but "trusted," they too can aspire to be as good as the superpowers. The language is reminiscent of the more overtly colonial past where subjects were required to take the curriculum and exams of their colonizers and to forget their own ways of knowing and education of their young (118). As we will see in the next section, another characteristic of this industry is key data and people moving across and between fields, including government, education, ranking and business.

The databases used by the Big Three

In November 2014, THEWUR announced that Elsevier would be its new data partner. Previously THEWUR was "powered by Thomson Reuters"; however, in the news release they explained that "going forward, all institutional data collection, previously outsourced to Thomson Reuters, will be expanded and carried out by a dedicated team of data analysts at THE" (119). Elsevier's managing director explains the partnership will work well because both THE and Elsevier are based in helping universities, industry, and government shape policy, strategic priorities, and make good investment decisions. Indeed the end of the news release assures universities that "we aim to help universities, funding bodies and governments establish and implement their strategies. We feel privileged to be playing an active role in helping universities calibrate their progress" (119).

Not surprisingly, unmentioned is the boycott against Elsevier by academics. Fourteen thousand nine hundred and seventy academics have signed a petition to boycott Elsevier for its high prices for journals that have caused hardship to university libraries, and have made the sharing of research a very expensive proposition. Many rankings use the Scopus database owned by Elsevier to determine a university's productivity. Indeed, many universities use journal rankings in their tenure and promotion processes, and so boycotting a monopoly may seem to be a dangerous proposition for faculty. Elsevier, Springer and Taylor & Francis make on average 18.9% in profits (120). Desiring greater profits, Elsevier lobbied hard for a bill that would have prohibited researchers receiving federal funds from the US to give free access to their research to the public. Under pressure, they eventually withdrew their support for the bill (121).

Academic journals are just a part of Elsevier's business. *The Lancet* published a letter from scholars concerned that the journal that was started to promote health and peace was owned by Reed Elsevier, which also "organised some of the world's largest arms fairs through its exhibition wing, Reed Exhibitions" (122: p. 889). The letter explained the apparent conflict of interest that is exacerbated by Reed Elsevier's own subscription to the UN Global Compact, which aims at preventing conflicts and human rights abuse.

A month after the THE–Elsevier news release stating they would be working in partnership, Thomson Reuters (TR) put out a release in December 2014: "Thomson Reuters Powers World's Leading University Rankings." Readers are told that TR is the power behind the "Times Higher Education, BRICS and Emerging Nations Ranking," *U.S. News and World Report's* Best Global University, ARWU and others. Readers are also told that it owns InCites™, "the world's leading research evaluation platform and home to Global Institutional Profiles, the benchmarking engine behind the Times Higher Education ranking." TR also "collaborates with many evaluation and policy groups around the globe" (123). It posted $12.6 billion for 2014 revenues (124).

TR has a number of software holdings, and has assets in the banking, mining, legal and tax sectors, and it also owns what was called the ISI and is now called the Web of Science. TR, also for a fee to universities, creates institutional profiles that provide comparative data for institutions to be used in the quest for improved rankings, as well as a product to benchmark, and to "compare and explore true and aspirational peers across a variety of indicators." Software to monitor staff and students is represented as essential for moving up in the rankings: "There has never been a more pressing need to demonstrate the impact and importance of your institution's research for promotion, development and funding purposes and there has never been a better way to do it than InCites" (125).

In a promotional video for "InCites," the audience is told they can "calibrate [their] strategic research vision" (125). InCites announces that it can be used to make decisions about what research will bring the greatest return on investment. The viewer first sees a satellite image of the globe – focusing in and out on different parts of the planet. The audience is then told, "Competition is at an all time high" (125). The video goes on to explain that there is greater scrutiny on funding decisions and pressure to improve performance by retaining top talent, and to demonstrate return on investment. To questions such as "Which program should I allocate resource?", "Who deserves promotion and tenure?" and "How can I attract the best and brightest?" (125), InCites responds that it provides "relative data and easy to use tools to evaluate institutions and departments" (125). InCites, like the QS lion, claims the capacity to overcome weakness and flaunt strength.

The narrator, with music in the background, assures viewers that InCites provides the rigorous and time-tested "gold standard" (125) metrics that will help them attain world-class status. The question of why universities need to purchase these products to maximize return on investment (ROI) is not part of the package. Instead, education's conflation with ROI is naturalized, as is the idea of decreasing the role of professional human judgment in hiring and tenure and promotion. The "Big Three" represent their work as monitoring and helping universities improve, but the question of who is watching these watchdogs is given far less attention by media and universities.

Movement of people across ranking organizations and sectors

The "Big Three" refer to three separate rankings, but they do not operate as separate enclaves: There is significant movement between rankings. It is this movement and the networks that come with it that suggest rankings form an economic sector. One of the more interesting things about this sector is how people move around in different capacities; for example, a number of advisory members for the "Big Three" and IREG move across and within the fields of government, business, media and HE. Many of the advisory members and staff have worked in business, government, media and academia. For example, the ARWU advisory board has nine members, seven with doctorates. Of these, four have academic appointments and others work in other areas (e.g., one member works with UNESCO and another the Observatory of Science and Technology in France). (See Appendix 2 for links to biographies of each advisory member on the four advisory boards.)

In 2009, after QS and THE parted ways, Phil Baty, who had worked for QS-THE and moved to be the editor of the new Times Higher Education World University Rankings (THEWUR), wrote a "Ranking Confession" for *Inside Higher Ed* that admitted the QS-Times Higher Education ranking was flawed and that rankings needed to be serious and go beyond annual curiosity. Baty cites a university president who was cynical about the split between QS and THE as a move to create more instability and keep communications at universities busy. What makes Baty's response especially interesting is that generally PR people advise executives to avoid providing credence to the other side by responding to their arguments, but to reframe the issue and offer their own arguments. But by providing such sharp criticism of the joint ranking for which he worked, and by using an academic detractor to present a counter-story, Baty attempts to persuade readers that criticism has been heard and the new ranking will be academically rigorous.

Phil Baty crosses sectors. Based on his biography, he was "named among the top 15 'most influential in education' by *The Australian* newspaper in 2012" (126). He also writes regularly for newspapers on education and was commissioned to write a report for UNESCO titled *Rankings and Accountability in Higher Education* (UNESCO). Here we see a high degree of mediatization: Baty, a journalist, has become one of the most powerful commentators, and arguably policy actors, on HEI.

Martin Ince also crosses sectors. On his website, written in a third-person authoritative voice, we are told that he has "long experience as a journalist, editor and author," and that this "means that there are few communications or media issues on which he cannot advise" (127). Readers are told he and his team make "tricky issues manageable." Notice how this phrasing subtly recasts higher education not as an endeavor or a field, but as a business, and one that faces the kind of complicated issues that require good messaging and issues management. However, Ince's company also offers the information of an insider: The reader is told that Ince remains the chair to the global Advisory Board for the QS World University Rankings and that "Martin now works with universities around the world that want to understand how rankings are produced, how they are used by a wide range of stakeholders, and how rankings status might be enhanced" (128). Absent is any discussion of how this work improves education. Similarly, no mention is made of possible conflicts of interests created by Ince being a consultant for universities wanting to know "How ranking status might be enhanced." The focus is making good business decisions.

Personnel differences are evident across the "Big Three." The QS has an advisory board with 28 people; the majority of the 12 academics on the board hail from business schools or STEM areas; however, there is one higher education specialist and two philosophers. Many are involved as consultants to industry and some as consultants to government. Four senior media people sit on the board, as well as others with a media background: For example, the advisory board includes Robert Morse, the editor of the *U.S. News and World Report* University Rankings in the US, a popular rankings and a partner of QS; John O'Leary, the former editor of the *Times Higher Education* and education editor of the *Times*; and Bhaskar Das, the former editor of the best-selling English paper in India, the *Times of India*. Academic staff who sit on the board work in communication, marketing and innovation, or have senior leadership positions at universities.

The TES board has a number of individuals who also cross fields. TES is most open in its connection to government with all of its members at some point involved in government policy and, in particular, policy around the privatization of education. For example, the board of TES includes Lord Puttnam, a trade envoy for the UK prime minister, a film producer (*The Killing Field* and *Chariots of Fire*), president of UNICEF UK and chairman of Atticus Education in Ireland; Lord Adonis, who was previously a journalist for the *Financial Times* and a former policy advisor for Tony Blair; Owen Lynch, former CEO of the British Educational Communications and Technology Agency and who served as a government consultant on education policy; and Baroness Morris, also a trade envoy and Chairman of the Conservative Middle East Council.

In November 2014, TES announced that a new TES Higher Education Board would be created and the Rt Hon David Willetts was named chair. Willetts was the minister of science in the UK and was "due to leave parliament" to become a visiting professor at King's College in London. Again the language of business and urgency is used: "He brings a wealth of knowledge about higher education at a time of rapid change, when the exchange of ideas, staff, students and funding is increasingly international in scope and scale" (129). As minister of universities and science, Willetts asserted that indicators of university performance would be linked to an understanding of students as consumers (129).

Advisory members often belong to more than one ranking organization or cross from one to another. Some members of ranking advisory boards also are part of The IREG Observatory on Academic Ranking and Excellence (in short: IREG Observatory) which was started in 2002 and defines its purpose as "strengthening of public awareness and understanding of a range of issues related to university rankings and academic excellence" (130). The Observatory includes "ranking organizations, universities and other bodies interested in university rankings and academic excellence." When IREG announced they would do audits of rankings, the head of "the intelligence unit at QS" Ben Sowter stated "There is a long way to go before this audit looks like the kind of measure it needs to be" (131). Robert Morse further explained that *U.S. News and World Report*, "would most likely participate in the audit, but only 'after we fully understand the processes and how it's going to be scored.'" He further hints that there is really no need for an audit since they already communicate "frequently with academics, but maybe we would need to also post in more detail about the mathematical processes and quality controls and other steps we take from the academic level, and that's something that we would consider doing" (131). Morse uses a rhetoric of certainty – his company understands what a scientific rank is and auditors would need to prove that they understood this as well. In 2013 QS became an important endorser of IREG, stating on its website: "Great news! QS has become the first compiler of global and regional university rankings to receive the 'IREG Approved' label for three of its research outputs" (132). The movement of people from one ranking organization to another, or from government to ranking organization, or from ranking organization to university consultant, might be seen as analogous to politicians retiring and thereafter using their networks to become lobbyists.

Representation and equity

All three rankers use a very similar language of excellence, reinforcing the appearance of consensus, and each presents claims of having the support of all categories of respondents, including students, making it appear that no one is opposed to the common-sense goodness of their rankings. But each of them leaves out voices that might challenge their representation of excellence.

At the time of my analysis (early 2015) of the "Big Three" and IREG websites, white males form a large majority among ranking advisory boards and staff, mirroring the leadership of many universities ranked as world class. The IREG Observatory Executive Committee, for example, is comprised of 12 people (nine men and three women). The president, Jan Sadlak, is on the advisory board for ARWU; Robert Morse is on the board of QS; and Nian Cai Liu is the head of ARWU. Seven members are from Eastern Europe and many are involved with setting up ranking systems in their respective countries. QS, TES Global and ARWU advisory boards are all male dominated (23 of 28, 4 of 5 and 7 of 10 respectively).

There is rhetoric of world-class institutions being places of innovation and free thinking for hungry, tech-savvy young people. QS paradoxically talks about the need to be innovative and empower the new generation of savvy and skeptical youth, yet its board is dominated by male elites, some of whom have been challenged for censoring skeptical students. Paul Wellings, vice-chancellor of Wollongong University in Australia, for example, was sharply criticized for actions he took as the vice-chancellor in Lancaster: He pressed for charges towards six students that peacefully protested a corporate venturing meeting at the university which included a number of companies involved in arms, and harmful human rights and environmental practices (133). A number of groups supported the students including civil liberties groups, the National Union of Students, and Scientists for Global Responsibility. Tsui Lap-Chee, the president and vice-chancellor of University of Hong Kong, was criticized for the Hong Kong University 818 incident in which he allowed a lockdown of the school during a visit of a government vice-premier in 2011 (134); his acceptance of the lockdown was seen as a slippery slope toward central government control of HKU and led to protests by students, faculty and journalists. Monique Canto-Sperber outraged many well-known academics, including Jacques Rancière, Etienne Balibar, Alain Badiou, as well as Judith Butler, Angela Davis and Gayatri Chakravorty Spivak, when, as director of École Normale Supérieure, she prohibited two events that were critical of the Israeli government (135, 136). Choosing advisory members who have been the object of sustained critique by academics but celebrated by industry and government raises questions about how the QS balances academic norms and the protection of corporate and government interests. What do the policies that advisory members initiate or support in their own institutions say about how they think about what and who the university is for? These protests also point to how students and others use media in attempts to resist the marketization of their institutions.

None of the three rankers measure a university's record or commitment to human rights, equity, treatment of indigenous peoples where the university is located, or environmental sustainability. Arguably a university that produces stacks of research on weapons of mass destruction, gets lots of money, and wins awards for their research can be a world-class university. Conversely, a university that successfully engages in equity seeking social and environmental ways of interacting with each other – within and outside the university – has no hope of such an honor.

Conclusion

The relationships among players in the education industry are dense and not always readily apparent. Different ranking organizations develop different contexts and have varying strategic aims and primary audiences: THEWUR comes out of a media company, QS a company specializing in study-abroad networks and business education, and ARWU a university. They have different stakeholders and pressures. However, all play a role in the mediatization of education. The indicators may be different, particularly between the ARWU and THEWUR and QS, but all three operate within the logics of mediatization and marketization of higher education: There is no room for ambiguity or nuance in determining quality; there are clear links between rankers and the development of various ancillary products; there is a clear cycle of profit based on the integration of rankings, spinoff products and other interests.

Rankings reflect larger tensions around local versus global geopolitics, and national and international pressures at the level of institutions and nations obsessed with nation branding to attract high-value students and faculty. However, there is also a great deal of convergence across the three rankings largely due to mediatization. This isomorphism is seen in, for example, the defining of "excellence" and "world-class" in similar ways; in the collection and use of comparable information; in the embedding of ranking in economic interests and the use the language of business standards; and in the movement of the same people across organizations. Indeed, this degree of convergence is even apparent in ranking organizations' constant need for something new to attract and maintain customers; as Bourdieu maintained, journalists need a scoop, but they must also mimic competitors (137). We do see a great deal of mimicry among the three in terms of spinoff products such as the BRICS ranking. This is particularly apparent in the competition between the QS and THEWUR.

In the next chapter, I will focus on the grammar of images through an analysis of the Times Higher Education World University Ranking website.

4
Visualizing Excellence: The Times Higher Education Ranking

The choreography of websites is based in a grammar of images. Of course, rules of grammar can and are often broken, but having a sense of the grammar of images and use of color that website designers employ is central to understanding visualization as part of marketization of higher education. This chapter will examine the Times Higher Education World University Rankings (THEWUR) website as a corporate media product *and* as a case study of the 2011–2012[1] (214) and the 2014–2015 rankings.

THEWUR rankings are the second most publicized ranking system, and are used by universities and media.[2] The focus of this chapter is not to claim there is a trend from 2011–2012 to 2014–2015, but to examine continuity and shifts in discourse. This chapter will first summarize literature related to website design, including uses of color and layout, and then analyze the use of advertising, external validators and modular rankings to maintain ongoing interest in THE products and compete with new products created by ARWU, QS and other rankers.

Website design

When a website is written in a language that moves from left to right, we should expect to see information that we as readers are expected to know on the left side (138). A center image, however, disrupts this flow and signals that something or somebody is important; the placement, color and size of an image is a significant indicator of importance. Framing is used to guide the reader in understanding how images and text fit together. As I will describe in this chapter, one of the most striking aspects of the THE 2011–2012 website is the use of highly saturated colors and animated narration, as compared to the 2014–2015 version's more subdued colors and authoritative voice.

The 2011–2012 THEWUR

The THEWUR page is vibrant. The colors – orange, fuchsia and blue – used to spell out the upper-case TIMES HIGHER EDUCATION WORLD UNIVERSITY RANKINGS reappear throughout the website. Under "THEWUR" is smaller text: "powered by Thomson Reuters." Identifying Thomson Reuters by name and image signals that THE ranking are done by a reputable name known by news consumers and academics that publish in Thomson Reuters journals. If the viewer looks to the sidebars, it is clear the THEWUR is integrated with other services; for example, there are advertisements for IDP,[3] which bills itself as "not just an agent" for students looking for placement services. IDP is also part owner of the profitable English language proficiency test, the IELTS, and also sponsors a widely distributed supplement about the benefits of the THEWUR for making good, personalized choices. THE allocates 30% for teaching and learning environment which includes 4.5% for staff-student ratio, 15% for a reputation survey, 6% ratio doctorate awarded to academic staff, 2.25% doctoral to bachelor ratio and 2.25% institutional income. Similar to the other two rankings, what is not considered is the substantial academic literature that shows the connection to learning and access, equitable teaching practices, institutional policies that facilitate social justice, listening and responding to the needs of diverse students, including community in learning and equity of opportunity among faculty.

If readers click on "Region," they are given the choices of Europe, Asia, North America, South America, Oceania or Africa. The bulk of institutions in the 1–200 range are in North America and Europe, with a few in Asia, and their scores are provided in eye-catching fuchsia. HEIs that don't make it into the top are not ranked, but referenced instead with the words "Data withheld by the THEWUR." If readers click on the "by Subject" tab, they will be given the choices of subject-based categories such as clinical and pre-clinical studies. Similar to the "by Region" category, there is no explanation of how categories were chosen or measured.

"Analysis": popular demand and the rise and fall of universities

The rules for measurement are obscure, but the language is one of certainty; the language of "analysis" and transparent and respected methodology is present throughout the site. There are ten pieces under "Analysis," three (accessed September 9, 2012) are written by Phil Baty, the Times Higher Education rankings editor. There is a hyperlink entitled "Ranking

Methodology," but the piece is entitled "Change for the Better" and Baty acknowledges that one ranking cannot be perfect, but that the THEWUR "can make bullish claims for the sophistication and utility of its annual World University Rankings." Critiques of past methodological flaws are addressed by telling the reader that the new rankings included "10 months of open consultation" which involved "50 leading figures from 15 countries." Readers are not told how experts and their nationalities were chosen to rank universities across the globe, but that "Last year's tables set a new standard, underpinned by a new methodology that quickly earned widespread acceptance and support." The tables are represented as actor; that is, the tables, rather than people with values and beliefs, reflect a new methodology that earned not just acceptance but widespread acceptance.

In looking at THEWUR, we see a focus on the role of Thomson Reuters Web of Science in determining the impact of scholars and institutions. THEWUR standardizes what is considered excellence through a focus on the market. Readers are told that Z-scores are used:

> The calculation of Z-scores standardises the different data types on a common scale and allows fair comparisons between different types of data – essential when combining diverse information into a single ranking (116).

Z-scores can of course be useful, but what is worthy of attention is how the language of research is used to gain legitimacy. Left unexamined is how and who makes decisions about what data should be collected and what beliefs and values underpin these decisions; numbers appear to speak a true story without the interference of human bias, values, beliefs and ideologies.

Further down the "Change for the Better" article, there is a pie chart with vivid colors, sparse words and numbers. The numbers in the pie chart construct the research as above financial or other interests; for example, readers are informed of the weighting for industry income, which measures how much a university receives from industry to sponsor research. Other ranking considerations include teaching and learning, citation and research influence, and research volume, income, reputation and international outlook. The indicators and weightings are presented as part of a seamless natural and social order. In "Under the Radar Activity," Phil Baty writes:

> The tables, published by popular demand and as part of our commitment to transparency, provide a valuable behind-the-scenes

insight....They allow a good view of national higher education systems, highlighting some that are perhaps in decline as well as those that are on the rise (139).

Baty uses language of "popular demand," but the public that has created this popular demand is not defined. Rhetoric of democratic, transparent information for making good educational decisions is used to obscure the fact that THEWUR is a media product with important economic implications for media outlets and universities. Democracy and branding are represented as one, rather than in tension, eliding THEWUR's aim to be both product and a policy driver. The product is advertised throughout multiple outlets and through agencies such as IDP that place international students; the rankings, however, as discussed in chapters 1 and 2, attempt to inform both student recruitment and government educational policy.

THEWUR is represented as a convergence of popular demand and transparency. Who is the public that forms the popular demand? Did parents and students en masse ask for tables? Was it media or universities? Who created the popular demand? Not only are the tables represented as responding to an imaginary public, but they purport to provide a transparent look at a national system. The tables, not people, provide objective information that helps individuals make choices. The tables tell universities and nations if they are on the "rise" or the "decline." The underlying logic is that what is popular is justified and true, and that the responsible person can empower her/himself to make the right educational decisions. Universities and governments can appear to make decisions not based on their own values and beliefs about what counts as education and what is important and valid research, but on the neutral data from THEWUR. Baty contrasts universities on the rise with those on the decline:

> The performance of Italy's universities is striking. Home to perhaps the oldest university in the Western world, the University of Bologna, Italy is notable for the absence of any of its institutions from the top 200 (139).

There are also the countries that could improve if only they adopted Western forms of governance: For example, the central claims made for the lackluster performance of China in the rankings are government management of higher education, lack of talented faculty, and a "fair and competitive environment for academics to perform excellently by international standards" (139).

Reputation

The tab next to "Analysis" is "Reputation," which again provides rankings as well as "analysis" and "methodology" as it applies to the reputation indicators of the rankings. Here again is the use of journalistic headlines and writing to explain the truth of the rankings, such as "Birds? Planes? No, colossal 'super-brands'", by Phil Baty. The icon of Superman taps into stories of greatness beyond dreams of the ordinary. Super-brands cannot be toppled, but they must still watch out for upstarts that aim to topple them.

Also, under "Reputation," the reader can click on the THEWUR table and quickly determine excellence by looking at which universities make the top 100. The use of the reputation indicator constructs a tautology of visibility: If institutions have the resources to pitch stories to the press and saturate the market with their brand, they will be more visible and more attractive to scholars, funders and students. Greater visibility might also encourage peer reputation evaluators to rank institutions based on how often they appear in various media. Nonetheless, those rankings are based on slim actual evidence: The response rate for the reputational survey is low. Furthermore, countries that are frequently exposed to THE products are over-represented (7).

Baty's discussion suggests that where one goes to school is tied to identity and democracy, which, in turn, are connected to the free market and the right to choose between products:

An American tale again, but this year with a twist: Caltech has deposed Harvard as world number one. Phil Baty explains that size is not everything in the rankings game…. Harvard – the world's best-known university, boasting a brand some sources rate as more valuable than Pepsi, Nike or Sony – has this year been pushed off the top spot (140).

Harvard may be a powerful brand, but it too can end up in a battle in a free marketplace of educational products. The irony of the analogy to the competition between Pepsi and Coke sets up the struggle that ends in one side pushed off its top spot. Even top brands can be toppled if universities play their cards right, as Phil Baty explains: "With focus, smaller teams can win big." Again, the focus is on being good at business and finding the right business niche as with any other product. The rankings show that maintaining market ground requires constant branding: Similar to Coke, Pepsi – and Thomson Reuters – universities need to stay on top of the THEWUR game to be represented as great schools.

Thomson Reuters and its many products, 2011–2012

The range of products that TR manages is not readily apparent on the THEWUR homepage; however, if readers click on the Thomson Reuters icon, they will learn it also produces a Top 100 Global Innovators ranking, and provides media, governance, risk and compliance consulting, Global HD video, financial information, Reuters Newswire and digital syndication. The THEWUR website also functions as a media site with space for advertisers to see their educational products. There are enticements for prospective advertisers. For example, potential advertisers are told that advertising in the THEWUR will yield results: "On an international basis, we get coverage from *Die Zeit, Le Monde, The Australian,* the *Times of India, XinMin,* News365.com and *The New Straits Times* to ensure the highest number of viewings for your promotion world wide" (141).

THE generates social and political capital by referencing media outlets carrying the rankings. However, a tautology is again at play: Information for prospective advertising outlets explains that THEWUR matters because respectable outlets cover its rankings and so, to attract advertising from products that aim to improve rankings, they too should cover THE rankings. THEWUR provides ways for advertisers, including universities, to increase their ranking and subsequent market share.

The THE website is focused on showing the rankings to be a reputable, transparent product that understands the needs of students for excitement and adventure – with a promising career at the end of the university road. The middle of THEWUR's homepage is the most brightly colored feature and includes a screenshot of a 2.55-minute video that reveals the "top 10 greatest universities in the world for 2011 to 2012." The video draws on the genre of a feature-length Hollywood film with a countdown that generates anticipation. Before the narrator reveals the "most comprehensive universal rankings ever" of "the top ten universities in the world for 2011–2012", however, he first asks "How do we measure greatness?". The answer is that "in order to measure greatness we measure a lot of different things."

Next, images of a ruler appear. The ruler sequence starts with three powerful metaphors symbolizing various aspects of greatness. First, the image of a shark appears representing uncontested power, strength, stealth aggression and cunning. The text at the top of the image reads "Great White Shark," but the shark is purple. The background looks like it is radiating energy, or perhaps a halo, to demonstrate the exceptionalism on display throughout the video. Second is the image of a map with the heading "Great Britain," epitomizing imperial scope, wealth, royalty, tradition – and universities that make these achievements possible. Human hierarchies become naturalized. Finally, an image of the "Great Wall of China" embodying stability and persistence. All three images reinforce that the top universities are beyond the everyday; they are – indeed – great. Using the symbols of the great white shark, Great Britain and the Great Wall of China, the narrator reinforces his message: "We measure a lot of different things. We measure things like the quality of teaching environment on offer." Here, the radiating sun or perhaps a halo turns pink to match the creation of a vibrant nature with a majestic building and flying, chirping birds in the background.

These images of greatness lead to the need to measure teaching excellence. Terms such as "culture of teaching excellence" are matched with images of teachers holding a trophy: "Did you know the University of Hong Kong fosters a culture of teaching excellence by holding an annual award ceremony for its staff? We did." Many universities bestow awards for teaching excellence, but the image of two happy-looking faculty members holding a large trophy represents superior teaching and working conditions. The iconography of the trophy provides a shortcut that does not invite the viewer to think about how the awards banquet at this university is different from others. More importantly, how a teaching banquet equates to recognizing the importance of teaching is not explained.

From the image of the trophy-holding faculty members, the narrator asks the audience: "Did you know we measure diversity? Did you know 28% of students from the University of Melbourne are international students…Who knew? We did." We then see an image of a white male with a ruler next to him. This focus on head measurement is reminiscent of the 19th-century science of phrenology and the early 20th-century theories of eugenics where human heads were measured to entrench nationalistic, racist and sexist ideologies. But now there are six heads that *represent* an imagined diverse public. There are no bodies. The white male looks bluish-white, and the five other heads appear to be colors of pink, green, orange and purple. National flags are superimposed the faces. Everyone appears happy and young. The use of different colors – not consistent with the human species – suggests a carefree diversity. The white privilege and colonialism of highly ranked HEIs is absent and, instead, technicolor invites prospective students to a land of joy and equity. Diversity is connected back to industry with the image of a power station and a bright blue sun motif; again the viewer sees the ruler on top. The narrator tells the audience, "We measure links with industry." The audience is not told on what basis the links are measured because the assumption is that links are always good for universities. The use of pink to represent a power station and science is interesting. Pink is a common color through the THE website (e.g., in the lettering of THE). The pink triangle was used by the Nazis in World War II to mark and humiliate LGBTQ+ people. The symbol was reappropriated to represent gay pride in the 1970s. Pink is often associated with femininity: Today, pink sometimes denotes "economic independent, hedonistic femininity" (142) and the punk singer Pink uses the stage name to critique gender politics (142). Pink in THEWUR, however, seems to provide a sense of fun that distracts from what might be a critique of focusing university success on power plants.

Images of research excellence then are connected to commercialization. "Did you know that MIT alumni helped Campbell's canned soup put the Technicolor in color and designed Gillette super smooth razors? We did." As this is narrated, a can of Campbell's Chicken Noodle Soup with a Gillette razor cutting through it is seen. Throughout the video, there is a center that appears to be a sun with rays of energy. The rays flicker and turn to different Technicolors. The rays appear to shine like a halo. MIT is known for its scientific innovation, so the choice of a smooth razor and soup labels as examples of stellar innovations seems surprising. Excellence is portrayed as the creation of everyday products that are discarded after one use, and have nothing to do with intellectual pursuits. A razor and a bowl of soup are mundane, but they are not controversial. However, many people can relate to shaving and almost everyone can relate to bowls of soup. The producers could have shown research that has resulted in "smart" bombs, or safer birth control, but these choices to represent research would be controversial; soup and razors are not controversial and mask the ideological underpinnings of representing research as neutral and commercial.

The word "research" first comes up at 1:04 minutes of the 2.55-minute video. An image of a beaker appears. The narrator states: "Finally we measure the importance of research being carried out at the university." It is noteworthy that research gets last mention because a university can only be considered great by the THE ranking if it is highly cited in research, has money and is considered to be worthy of high ranking by peers.

A theme throughout the video is "Who knew? We did." The audience is reminded constantly that only the THEWUR has access to knowledge that allows them to tell the audience how to make the right choices. The assumption is that the audience will learn more through the ranking than other means of learning about the strengths and limitations of different institutions. The images with the ruler described earlier reappear at the beginning of the countdown. The narrator states that the Times Higher Education ranking is the most comprehensive in the world: "So, now you know a bit about how we know what are the greatest universities in the world." We are brought into an understanding of what appears to be an incontrovertible, uncontested truth about the top universities in the world. The countdown images reappear as well, but this time in color. A university is announced and its masthead appears.

> The Greatest University in the world for 2011–2012 IS....
> There is a pause in narration and a drumroll....
> The UNIVERSITY OF CALTECH!!!!
> If you want to know more why not explore the university rankings website today?

The metaphors, such as the Great Wall or the great white shark, employed along with tables, reinforce THEWUR's representation of truth. The table visually signifies the verified truth needed to make individual, institutional or national choices. Explanations of movement up or down the ranking scale connect back to the primacy of capitalism as central to educational quality. Baty, for example, explains that some Eastern European universities, although not in the top 200, should feel hopeful. The hope is not based on their own efforts, but because the European Union has helped them internationalize by fully embracing capitalism and the entrepreneurial university.

Branding THEWUR in 2014–2015

Fast forward to 2014–2015 and THEWUR has new products – and new competitors – and instead of being "powered by Thomson Reuters" they use the language of outsourcing to Elsevier. In 2015 there is the same THE logo with the same colors, and the same format for the ranking tables with the score for the first 199 universities shown in bright pink and 201–500 accompanied only with the text "Data Withheld." But there are some significant differences too.

In 2014, instead of Technicolor, there are subdued images of balloons moving skyward that cue readers that they are not on the world university ranking page, but on the BRICS and Emerging Economies ranking page. Color schemes can be seen as connected to historic moments; for example, "the postmodern color scheme, based on hybridity and pastel values." However, color schemes also "move beyond their historical period as recognized semiotic resources which can continue to be used and combined...to realize distinctly different ideological positions" (138: p. 366). In the THE site, we see different color schemes that are deployed alongside semantic resources to categorize universities from the "top of the pile" to the "wannabes" (22).

Instead of the Technicolor of 2011–2012, viewers are now greeted by a well-known British journalist, Rageh Omaar, who is interviewing Phil Baty on the steps of an imposing Greco-Roman building (part of the academic quad at the University College London). We are not told who Omaar is, other than he is a broadcaster, but in fact he is a well-known former BBC and Al Jazeera award-winning journalist. His international background and credibility as a journalist provides credibility to his interview with Phil Baty and an appearance of independent validation of the THEWUR. The tone is that of a serious journalist doing the investigative work to help students and families make good choices. There is no sign of questioning or uncertainty in his voice; after all, he is revealing the ten greatest universities in the world. Koh points to the power of documentary to eliminate representation of the messiness of educational policy: "The old adage that says 'what-you-see-is-what you get' works powerfully to dissuade us from believing otherwise" (143: p. 294).

The video is 9.52 minutes. Similar to 2011, the audience is told how THEWUR works with academics, compares tens of thousands of data points and can be trusted because the ranking has an eleven-year track record. We are also told academics and policymakers use rankings, but the most important audience is parents and students who need to know whom to trust with their future. Omaar appears to be an objective reporter who is giving parents and students information they need to know to make good choices.

Baty is clear that THEWUR ranking is credible, partly because "We have being producing for over a decade" and "We have an incredibly long and detailed experience." This is interesting given Baty's previous admission that THE and QS separated in 2009 because of disputes about methodology. Viewers are also assured that the ranking looks at the entire portfolio of university responsibilities, including knowledge transfer, research, international outlook and "teaching environment." Absent is any attention to local community or the needs and interests of the particular context in which a university is located. "Tens of thousands of data points are collected": Data is again naturalized as something good, concrete and objective and collecting information replaces academic norms of analysis, interpretation and peer review. All that is needed is an explanation of how and what is collected and assurance that the analysis provides responsible consumers with what they need to know.

The language of needing to know is again used. When asked why the ranking is so popular, Baty explains that students are spending tens of thousands and so "they need to know and they need the reassurance they are going to a world-renowned university. The degree or certificate is almost a global passport for their future career success." The implication is that the vast majority of students in the world who do not get into world-class universities are destined to a life of failure.

There is no longer a countdown clock or animated Technicolor scheme, but now THEWUR, Baty tells viewers, has developed a new business index to judge HEIs. Students need to know how what they learn is applied to the "real world", and the "real world" is clearly the business world. The video starts with regions of the world at the bottom of the ranking, but it tells viewers they have potential and some are moving up, e.g., the University of São Paulo in Brazil which hasn't quite made the top 200. We are told they haven't internationalized enough like others in emerging economies, but "it is on the up." There is no image of a ruler as there was in 2011–12, but language of countries inching forward towards improvement. The University of Cape Town, viewers are told, has pockets of excellence such as in astrophysics. And for Oceania, it is a "Mixed picture," with New Zealand not doing well and the University of Melbourne creeping its way up – with the "highest scores for international outlook." The only time the viewer is cued to the interviewer's experience is when he asks about the Middle East; Omaar states he is "particularly interested in Middle East because he spent time there." Again he tells us the picture is mixed, but if Turkey is included things look a bit better. The language of Asia rising is used, but in the end Omaar tells viewers, "The world's very best universities remain concentrated in Europe and particularly in the US." The conflation of Europe and the US is curious, but what brings both together is a dominance in defining what a world-class university should be.

THEWUR is no longer "powered by Thomson Reuters," but instead, next to the THE logo, in light small letters, viewers are told the ranking is "in partnership with ELSEVIER." The background color is a grayish-black. There are also new spinoffs or modular rankings on the homepage, including the THE "2014" ranking which was published in December 2013, the same year as the QS BRICS ranking; the THE BRICS ranking is visualized through a green Jack-and-the-Beanstalk-type growing plant with yellow hot-air balloons. Plans for the MENA ranking – Middle East and

North Africa – were announced in Qatar in February 2015; a pictur-esque scene accompanies the announcement with an ornate museum in Doha, Qatar. One of two other rankings that were around in 2011–2012 – the 100 Under 50 – has a beige and white image of a yellow, blue, green butterfly emerging from a cocoon. The other – the World Reputation Rankings – has a theme color of pink and an image of a cartoon male figure with a beard holding up a pen, and looking at the stars; he seems to be contemplating his decision about the next university "stars."

The process depicted on the website seems to promote the THEWUR brand as one that can be trusted. The language of revealing "world-class" universities appears throughout the website and is often paired with language of superbrands, transparency, research methodology and experts; for example, one of the pieces asserting the absolute cred-ibility of THEWUR is entitled "The formula for a world-class univer-sity revealed." Underneath the headline is what appears to be a male figure writing formulas on a whiteboard including $E=mc^2$ (144). How theories of special relativity determine which universities offer an excel-lent education remains unclear.

Learning from Walmart

Similar to 2011–12, there is frequent use of the language of sports reporting, but ironically, there is also a curious remix of business language with ancient Greek philosophy: Socrates is often deployed in ways that might baffle most philosophers. For example, images of a bust of Socrates adorn a page with an article titled, "That petrol, emotion," written by the former executive of Walmart and current director of corporate affairs at Sheffield, Nick Agarwal. Citing Socrates, he explains, "The way to gain a good reputation is to endeavour to be what you desire to appear" and "Let him that would move the world, first move himself" (145). From this premise the audience is told that to appear good requires more than just being good; it requires "a clear narrative that demonstrates it, and your stakeholders have to understand it, believe it and be prepared to endorse it to others." Education is an issue of pleasing "stakeholders" – not students or citizens. The clear narrative is associated with the neces-sity and goodness of capitalism: "An intellectual foundation is not enough: The narrative needs to engage the emotions, too. Nowhere was this clearer to me than during my time working for the US retail giant Walmart" (145). Agarwal goes on to suggest HEIs, like Walmart, care about people and so need to tell people how great they are: "The reality is that universities are deeply involved in the human condition: we should not be shy of saying how and why" (145). There is no sense of irony that Walmart, a company that fought against affordable health care in America, and against workers' right to organize, is used as an example of something to aspire to in understanding the human condition.

Socrates also appears in a piece written by Baty entitled "Credit Check" (146), but this time Simon Marginson, a well-known HEI scholar, is added as an external validator as Philip Altbach was in 2011. The article defends the use of the reputation survey indicator used by the THEWUR:

> "Reputation can be affected by marketing, rumour and factors from outside the sector, but it cannot be faked," Marginson, now at the Institute of Education, has said. Or as Socrates put it: "The way to gain a good reputation is to endeavour to be what you desire to appear."

Marginson is on the ARWU advisory board and he has expressed concern about reputation surveys (147). One can only guess what Socrates, famously quoted for saying, "The only true wisdom is in knowing you know nothing," would think of rankings. There continues to be frequent language of fact: "Matter of opinion? Try matter of fact" (148). The article explains that the world reputation survey "is likely a harbinger of things to come" and that "Phil Baty discovers the US remains the undisputed superpower when it comes to academic prestige." The language of discovery brings forth surprise; however, is it a surprise that the World Reputation Rankings placed the US at the top, given every ranking since the beginning – ARWU, THE and QS – has done so? The language is also naturalized. What decisions led to rankings being a harbinger? This article, like others, explains that reputation is crucial for HEIs, but the role of ranking in the reputation race is not interrogated.

In an article titled "Ebb and Flow on honour roll" (149) Baty tells readers,

> If a week is a long time in politics, four years is an age in terms of global university brands. In the image below we compare the position of institutions in 2011's inaugural World Reputation Rankings with today's figures to see whose esteem has risen or fallen the most.

Below this quote is a timeline that shows the movement of universities up and down the reputation stream. The connection to politics and branding is treated as common sense, thereby linking academic, political and corporate logics. The language is that of the natural ebb and flow, defined as "a condition or rhythm of alternate forward and backward movement or of alternate decline and renewed advance" (150); esteem rises and falls naturally. There seems to be an unexamined tension between the need for universities to provide stability to think and contemplate (once seen as the hallmark of a university) while constantly rising and falling in the public arena.

The language of disrupters and disruption was not evident in 2010–2011, but occurs in a number of 2014 articles. Disruption has often been used by activists to discuss strategies such as culture-jamming, aimed at challenging dominant discourses of capitalism and war. Here, however, we see the language co-opted in support of global brands. For example, the president of MIT, Rafael Reif, writes an article titled "Creative disrupters are welcome," telling the story of "Bhave," a "17-year-old from a small city in India" who took a MOOC from MIT and collected materials from online sources to create a follow-on course for himself and others. He subsequently joined the MIT class of 2017. Reif concludes:

> In some ways, the most striking aspect of Bhave's story was his simple refusal to accept the status quo, his conclusion that if the world was not providing something he needed, he would use the tools at hand to hack the present and produce the future of his dreams. This is the irreverent, do-it-yourself spirit that has inspired generations of MIT inventors and entrepreneurs. And it is the spirit of creative disruption that has made our campus one of the most productive sources of innovation in the world. In welcoming Bhave, we welcome him home to a community always hungry to learn, create and share (151).

Unquestioned is how it is that MIT is welcoming him "home". Is India a place that cannot sustain intellectual stars? If so, why? With the return, what happens to community and family? Were they figments of a developing imagination now ready to assimilate – to be home – in a developed country? What type of innovation or what "innovation" means is not spelled out.

Another article, "Perfect Pairings" (152), is illustrated with an image of seven people in white lab coats; one appears to be white and the others Asian. Anne Pakir, the director of International Relations for the National University of Singapore (NUS), explains how NUS has benefitted from partnerships with Duke and Yale and how this provides NUS with:

unique opportunities to leapfrog on to the top table of global universities. Through the synergies between the university and its partners – bodies that share the same vision and culture of innovation, and offer a distinctive value proposition to the world – Singapore's top institution has benefited hugely (152).

The desirability of being like an American university is assumed and therefore to "leapfrog" is reported as a rare opportunity for rapid development.

Glyn Davis, the vice-chancellor for the University of Melbourne, writes an article, "Excellence in Triplicate," that begins with an image of what appears to be the back of a man's head along with a compass and image of a cell. He explains that the university's high ranking is due to aligning itself to the finest European institutions, and "Since 2008, we have taught the Melbourne curriculum, which is closely based on the Bologna Declaration," and then claims:

> Melbourne's success has been 160 years in the making, and the challenge to continue improving is ever present. However, meeting that challenge is one way of ensuring – as the title of our Growing Esteem strategy suggests – that the university continues to serve the needs of future generations (153).

The THE website contains numerous references to third-party validation of THEWUR; for example, Baty informs readers that THEWUR was praised in "an influential House of Lords committee report that stated that a European Commission effort to create the U-Multirank might be "a waste of taxpayers' money" and that until the deficiencies can be overcome, "we consider that the Commission should prioritise other activities. In the meantime, rankings such as the Times Higher Education World University Rankings may have a valuable contribution to make" (154). Baty's narrative is one of constant improvement and responsiveness towards policymakers and academics – and that government efforts at subsidizing U-Multirank are a waste of public money. His view is then affirmed by the UK Minister of State for Universities and Science and current chair of the TES Higher Education Advisory Board, David Willetts, who is reported as telling THE that U-Multirank "could be viewed as 'an attempt by the EU Commission to fix a set of rankings in which [European universities] do better than they appear to do in the conventional rankings'" (154).

Advice for a price

Baty, perhaps the most prolific of the major rankers in advising governments and universities, admits that university rankings are influenced
by media. In explaining the decline in ranking for Australia in 2014, for
example, he is quoted as stating:

> *Times Higher Education* cannot know for sure, however, because
> the brand rankings are based on the subjective opinions of 10,000
> researchers from around the world. [However] right at the very time
> people were being asked to evaluate universities around the world
> there was a fairly dramatic piece of news coming out of Australia with
> negative implications (155).

Baty does go on to say public funding cuts could cause more slippage, but
counters this with private institutions that can stay consistent because
they are not dependent on government.

There appears to be continual product and spinoff product development, including conferences that are branded as "exclusive." I clicked on
the Young Universities Summit page within the Times Higher Education
website and was informed that:

> We would be honoured if you would register to attend this pres-
> tigious event. The Young Universities Summit, attended by univer-
> sity Presidents, Vice-Chancellors and Rectors, will feature speakers
> and panelists from top institutions across the globe, as well as the
> leaders of multinational corporations, government officials and poli-
> cymakers (156).

The conference is a two-day event at the cost of 600 GBP for university and 1,200 GBP for corporate participants. The conference homepage
promises "an exclusive first look at the 2015 THE 100 Under 50 results"
and an "exclusive rankings master class with Mr. Phil Baty, editor at
large and rankings editor, THE." The webpage explains:

> The event is part of the THE World Summit Series which includes
> THE World Universities Summit, the THE Africa Summit, the THE
> MENA Summit and the THE Asia Universities Summit. Because of the
> summit's exclusive nature, places are strictly limited: representatives
> from many universities and companies have already shown interest
> and demand is growing (156).

The language of exclusivity and the need to act now is clear.

Implied responses to critiques

Much of the THE's ranking website includes implied responses to critiques of the rankings. For example, Baty invokes well-known higher education scholar Philip Altbach to explain why government cuts give private institutions a better chance of being in the Top 10, but unmentioned is Altbach's (2012) critique of the methodological and conceptual underpinning of the rankings. Similar to amassing social and economic capital by reference to publications like *Le Monde*, deploying Altbach's name provides academic capital to the THEWUR enterprise.

The visions of scientific rationality, and the genres used – statistical tables along with pictures of happy students, beautiful campuses and cheerful faculty – tell the audience that the rankings are transparent. The rankings play into existing narratives about who are knowers and the beneficiaries of knowledge; women, racialized scholars and scholars with visible disabilities are absent or shown as outliers rather than with the norm. Indeed, part of the appeal of rankings is that they reinforce narratives of long-standing hierarchies within universities and media rather than challenging them.

THEWUR acknowledges the language of academic research – but uses this language in the context of mediatization. What is characterized as rigorous and comprehensive research is situated within the parameters of an annual news event for the World University Rankings and a number of other events for sub-rankings such as the World Reputation Rankings. Media logic dictates what can be measured and shown as proof of excellence within the time constraints of a news event. Throughout the THEWUR website, there is the presence of academic language of rigor, but power relations are submerged through visual framing that presents a world of choice for all who take the effort to properly choose. Numbers seem to create meaning by themselves without humans mediating what to count, how counting happens or what is understood from what we count. Images on the THE website act as powerful symbolic tools in a mediatized higher educational environment: The site promotes a reality where all that is good in higher education can be measured and hence visualized in an easily understood pie chart or colorful table.

The THEWUR website combines visuals of mobility in an international globalized environment. Tables are powerful images that can be quickly consumed as evidence of what are good and bad choices, and images of happy young people show the reward of making good choices. Data is presented as neutral information that serves decision-making from the individual to the government levels. Indeed, data becomes merged with tropes of democratic and transparent decision-making, eliding debate about what education is and could be and promoting instead a singular narrative of educational excellence as primarily Western and for economic gain. National governments can then use rankings to defend what appears to be a neutral, transparent and democratic allocation of resources; missing are the reasons for making decisions that often replicate or increase historical, colonial inequities.

Conclusion

A prospective student can click a mouse or swipe a finger on a mobile device to predict their future: Numbers provide objectivity and the images of happy students provide reassurance that the social capital acquired by students who choose the right university will lead to good lives. In sum, individuals can determine their future – as long as they use the rankings to make responsible, good educational choices. Mazawi (157) shows how the language of "responsibilizing the self" is part of the larger move of states to cut services and deregulate markets. In a consumer rather than equity framework individuals become responsible for the choices they make and therefore are at fault if they make bad choices. Attaining an education is depicted as a process of individuals working to better themselves through smart lifestyle and work choices. Within this spectacle, the role of the individual is to visualize her/his success and work to achieve this vision; the self becomes the unit empowered to create personalized policies. Absent is any reference to the economic or social capital needed to attend universities deemed to be of the highest quality.

Visuals representing excellence, quality and choice create the impression of a level global playing field, but analyzing the underlying logic of these representations of excellent higher education requires examining absence as well as presence. Missing on the THEWUR homepage, for example, is content about fields that are not deemed profitable or easily monetized such as teacher education, most social sciences, humanities, community-engaged scholarship, and indigenous knowledge. Absent also is the increasing cost of higher education and the impact this has on the choices that are available for poorer students. Understanding choosing a university as analogous to favoring Coke or Pepsi narrows selection criteria to considerations of preference and price. The comparison with products such as Campbell's and Gillette also points to the underlying logic of the THEWUR – higher education is something to be bought like any other product. What is ranked by the THEWUR is hugely influenced by multinational news networks that play key roles in framing the parameters for what is understood as educational excellence.

5
Mediatization and University Websites

Before becoming an academic, I was a communications director; my background followed me, and so I was soon asked to assist my department in redesigning its website. I was excited by Google Analytics,[1] a program that allowed me to go on my department's website and see how much time people spent on different webpages. Did changes to a webpage increase traffic? Tools such as Google Analytics allow universities to have a constant answer to "how do I look?" Am I still the fairest/ most world class in the land? Or translated, how many students are applying – is the number up from last year? What do stakeholders think of our brand? Do visitors to the site search for "ranking" or "financial aid" or "media experts"? How can we change our site to increase traffic? Oh, and in the excitement of colorful lines showing increasing or decreasing traffic, I almost forgot to ask "How does traffic connect to our reason for existing?"

Marketing in the HE sector is not new, particularly in an American context; for example, view books have been used, as well as filmstrips and CDs, to market HEI, but all communication was one way and fully controlled by the producers. University websites are places of cultural production: Through the multimedia of website design there are sets of representations, iconography and meanings about what universities stand for and, in consequence, branding through websites involves economic, cultural, and political activities. Websites provide a multimedia expression of the structure of an institution – and are also central to maintaining or increasing a university's market share as producers of knowledge and educators of the next generation.

In this chapter, I will analyze universities' websites in relation to the interwoven ways cultural and economic languages characterize websites. How do top-ranked universities communicate their identities through websites? Do we observe divergent imagery or increased homogeneity in how university websites communicate their cultural identities? Do we notice commonalities across contexts and sites that give weight to the argument of an emerging global visual language and political aesthetic of higher education?

Analyzing the design of websites of top national or international universities can provide us a useful window into the mediatization of higher education. A university website tells us much about what producers consider important, based on how many clicks it takes a reader to get to the content they desire. It also tells us about the aesthetic politics of the university: How does the institution use visual forms? If recruitment of international students is important to a university, for example, we would expect that international students will find it easy to learn how to apply. If universities are under increased pressure to fundraise, we could expect this to be represented on the website in different ways and we can analyze connections between economics, aesthetics and politics in the choices made around website design. A university may attempt to have centralized control over all webpages that appear on the university website; however, departments can also use tools such as Google Analytics to track users and build a sense of their target audiences. Through this process, departments may also shift priorities and target the most promising prospective student markets.

How are university websites similar and different across different contexts?

To explore this question, 13 websites of top-ranked universities in six countries – Canada, China, India, South Africa, the UK and the US – are analyzed. Obviously these six countries are positioned very differently on the world stage. The UK, the US and Canada are G8 economies; furthermore, many of the universities referred to in this chapter, unlike their counterparts, enjoy massive endowments. The universities in the UK and US consistently dominate the rankings, but many have also experienced massive cuts in public funding. In consequence, they now must compete with each other and other countries such as Australia to attract domestic students and recruit international students from the burgeoning middle and upper classes of countries such as India and China. At the same time, China, India and South Africa themselves are experiencing massive growth in HEI, and they too seek international students, mainly from other parts of Asia and Africa.

What to analyze?

For each country, the reader will note a short statement on the context of higher education. This is clearly not exhaustive, but provides a brief context to rankings in six national contexts. To create meaningful comparisons between websites, I limit my analysis to the *homepage* and references to rankings throughout the 13 websites. The homepage of a university website is where the brand strategy is most evident (158). Website designers often use language of newspapers: For instance, "above" and "below" the fold, reminiscent of how newspaper editors prioritized stories by placing them at the top of the page, i.e., "above the fold." It is these stories a prospective newspaper buyer first sees and which are key to attracting readership. Stories of less interest or stories aimed at a smaller group will most likely be placed "below the fold," along with contact information. Of course, there is no fold on a website, but for websites "above the fold" stories do not require the reader to scroll down.

The homepage is also a window into how the institution positions itself in relation to key indicators used by rankers such as research productivity and percentage of international students. For the present chapter, data collected during December 2014 is analyzed; using December as the month for capturing website data provides an opportunity to see how universities sum up the calendar year. These snapshots of the year in review are useful in exploring what different institutions see as their key successes over a year. (See Appendix 1 for description of methodology.) I also searched the entire websites of the 13 universities for mention of rankings, which provides information on how top-ranked institutions communicate ranking results to their own members and to external audiences. In particular, I was looking for university press releases, policy documents, and speeches from university leaders and governance bodies.

Color choices are not entirely local or global (138). However, increasingly Getty image bank graphics, as discussed in Chapter 1, are found throughout corporate, government, media and university websites. Colors are used to denote a sports team, a country or a cause – such as green for the environment and pink for breast cancer. Car companies legally protect their colors so that others can't use them (138). In my analysis of rules written by universities about use of their brand, clear direction was given on the use of color as part of brand protection strategies, as well as placement of logos, and dimensions to be used.

There are huge differences in the geopolitical placement of each country and, based on this, which universities can attract which students, faculty, staff and investors; furthermore, different histories affect how governments and universities interact. Are these differences evident in the websites of top-ranked universities in each nation? To better understand these questions, I provide a brief context for each country before launching into an analysis of university websites.

Canada

In Canada, *Maclean's* magazine produced the first media-created ranking of Canadian HEIs in 1990. Canadian HE is governed by provincial legislation; however, the federal government has taken an increased interest in education as an economic driver. In 2011, for example, the federal government announced that education would be part of the government's Economic Action Plan: "In a highly competitive, knowledge-based global economy, ideas and innovation go hand in hand with job creation and economic growth. In short, international education is at the very heart of our current and future prosperity" (159: p. 4).

The plan includes focusing on key markets and "includes a commitment to 'brand' Canada to maximum effect. This means refreshing our excellent value proposition for international education and developing appropriate promotional tools, such as customized marketing strategies that more powerfully target messages to potential students" (159: p. 4). "World class learning" is one of the headings in the plan and is supported with a reference to an OECD report that gives Canada a high ranking for education. To focus on world university rankings, however, limits the number of institutions eligible to become part of "Imagine Education au/in Canada" – a brand created by a partnership that includes the Canadian Ministers of Education and the Federal Department of Foreign Affairs, Trade and Development. Its aim is to increase the number of K–12 and post-secondary international students and express "empowered idealism" (160). Canadian HE and internationalization often references Australia as a country to emulate; Australian universities have on average 20% international students.

Canada is the only country in which the same university – University of Toronto (U of T) – is consistently ranked number one by ARWU, QS and THE. Internationally, U of T is ranked #20 by THEWUR and QS, and #24 by ARWU. For the sake of comparison, I've included the University of British Columbia (UBC), which is often ranked #2 in Canada; internationally UBC is ranked #33 by THEWUR, #43 by QS, and #37 by ARWU. In its own material, UBC just lists its rankings for THEWUR and ARWU (162).

University of Toronto and University of British Columbia

The University of Toronto homepage in 2014 is similar to a newspaper in terms of content organization. "Above the fold" is an image and text, "Meet our 2015 Rhodes Scholars: Meet Caroline Leps and Moustafa Abdalla" (163). Appearing next to the text is an image of a smiling young woman standing in front of a brick wall, and a smiling young man with the city behind him.

The language is of discovering U of T and of possibility along with budget tools and information about financial aid. A group of students lean over a lit board – all look happy and excited at whatever it is they are discovering. Mobile students are also a theme; a box labeled "U of T Global" includes an image of a white male against a blue sky background with one hand shading his eyes, like a soldier looking into the distance. At the bottom is information for internal members. Under "About U of T," rankings are not mentioned, but superiority is: Readers are told that the University of Toronto was established in 1827 and that it "has one of the strongest research and teaching faculties in North America, presenting top students at all levels with an intellectual environment unmatched in depth and breadth on any other Canadian campus" (164), a claim supported by another article that leads with a chart comparing U of T, UBC and McGill (each symbolized by its animal mascot). The chart shows U of T ranked ahead of its competitors above the text: "It was another banner year for the University of Toronto on the slate of international university rankings released this past fall." The use of the chart, mascots and banner suggests sports league standings, an impression reinforced by the announcement from Meric Gertler, U of T's president, that the U of T is "pleased to be recognized once again as the premier university in Canada, and to be named among the world's very best." Underneath are related stories on rankings – all showing that U of T is "best." Information about the ranking of U of T's Ontario Institute for Studies in Education appears under "About OISE." The dean comments on a QS ranking that gives OISE the #1 position for public institutions in North America and #9 position in the world: "I am pleased to see OISE faculty recognized again for our significant role in education research and knowledge mobilization. These results show that OISE is Canada's brain trust in education." "Brain trust" makes it clear that OISE needs to be protected like a bank; without OISE the country would lose the most important, trusted brains in Canada. Clearly, rankings are represented as external validators of excellence.

The discourse of entrepreneurship dovetails with discourses of innovation, personal choices and the knowledge economy. U of T "2014 in review" includes "our 5 biggest entrepreneurship stories" and "*Entrepreneurship* happens here." The images provided of "leading entrepreneurs" show six separate small images about different projects; in total there are 18 men and three women. All look happy, and include the stereotypical hipster-appearing young men with facial hair, nerds with plaid shirts, and, to the side, two young women. We see many of the same themes on the UBC website, but a different aesthetic.

The UBC homepage is unique in showing images with no anchoring text. A solitary encircled black-and-white image adorns the center of the page, and when viewers click on the image they are taken to a library of other black-and-white images that have recently been on the UBC website. With a click, most of the images turn to color. The images of students are most prevalent, and they embody popular iconic cultural symbols and signs. For instance, the first image is of the UBC Sororities President who has long hair that appears to be blowing in the wind; we are told she is passionate about people and diversity and that the sororities provide empowerment for women and self-development. Next we see a PhD student in math with long dreadlocks that seem to be blowing in his face; he is a "coffee enthusiast." Also appearing is a journalism student dressed to look like the comic character Clark Kent, who works as a journalist until he must turn into Superman to save the world from yet another calamity; we are told that he hosts a radio program and is "a tardy journalism student." The use of cultural icons is common throughout the site. The images and the short stories are skillful marketing messages that connect being a student with fun, an exciting lifestyle and personal development – a radical break from conventional images of universities populated with serious students in stuffy libraries. UBC students are not joining a stuffy ivory tower, but invited to an adventurous metamorphosis that will result in a light-hearted hybrid identity – fun-loving coffee drinkers who are committed to personal development and social justice. There appears to be no boundaries to the combinations (165).

Click on "About UBC," and the viewer sees a panoramic image of the campus, with a view of the ocean and a relatively old building on campus with the Ladner clock tower in the foreground, but the focus is on the physical beauty of the location, not its historical context. Underneath the image, viewers are told that "The University of British Columbia is a global centre for research and teaching, consistently ranked among the 40 best universities in the world." Like U of T, rankings play a role in UBC's self-promotion (161). Here we see that both U of T's and UBC's narrative is related to their position nationally and globally, with reminders of their respective histories; however, the imagery on both websites is of predominately young, white students who appear to be having fun.

China

In the 1990s, China implemented significant educational policies including Project 211 and Project 985, both aimed at creating world-class Chinese universities (166) partly by shifting higher education to private institutions with an emphasis on fundraising and tuition fees (167). In 2003, the Shanghai Jiao Tong University published its first rankings, now known as the Academic Rankings of World Universities (ARWU), which set up a new dynamic for HEIs. Countries like the USA and UK, previously confident in their high status, were put on notice with the creation of the ARWU. First, both international and Chinese students could now compare universities across contexts to decide where to attend. Second, the ARWU and government policies signaled that China planned to become an economic competitor, and part of its strategy involved building globally competitive universities. Government policies and rankings reflected geopolitics where comparison is at the forefront. In China, where all education is controlled by the national government, 39 leading Chinese universities were assigned additional funds to work towards world-class status (167); Peking and Tsinghua are among the highest funded in this group. To increase efficiency and competitiveness HEIs were merged to improve rankings (168) by, for example, giving Chinese academics in the West lucrative contracts to encourage them to return to China.

In 2014, ARWU ranks Peking and Tsinghua University in the group of 100–150 best universities; QS ranks Tsinghua #47, and the THEWUR gives Peking #48 in its rankings. Moreover, the BRICS (Brazil, Russian, India, China, South Africa) QS and THEWUR are dominated by Chinese universities (169). Arguably, China is moving closer to Western universities than universities in other emerging economies.

Tsinghua University and Peking University homepages

The first thing that struck me about the Peking University (PKU) and Tsinghua sites is that both include English and Chinese versions, yet the only official language of China is a dialect of Mandarin. (In contrast, Canada is officially bilingual – French and English – yet the University of Toronto and UBC have only English on their websites.) Given that China could choose from over

200 living languages native to China, the choice of English is worthy of exploration. Tsinghua's English and Chinese homepages have the same layout and image of what appears to be a young woman holding her parchment with two family members. In contrast, PKU has different content and images for the Chinese and English pages. The English version shows a large ornate room where a conference appears to be taking place; we can only see the speaker on the screen and the backs of heads. The focus is the grandeur of the room. Both the PKU and Tsinghua websites emphasize building relationships with the West, particularly America. Included on the PKU homepage, for example, is an image of the US Ambassador to China with the Mayor of Los Angeles beside a story describing business relationships between the US and PKU; a lecture about the shared history of the US and China is also highlighted. Below the fold we see color images of students and, below this, contact and other information.

PKU's English website is focused on PKU as world class and welcoming of international students and emphasizes individual aspiration, fun, and adventure. Its ranking is not mentioned, but instead its history and prestige and its excellent library. The order of information provides cues to what is seen as key information to communicate to audiences outside of China – in particular, Western audiences. In contrast, the Chinese version of the PKU site is more text heavy; there is one picture of a professor delivering a lecture and the text stresses the reputation of the university and its history. The Chinese version also includes information about meetings as well as administrative, academic and political issues.

My first look at the Peking University Chinese site was perplexing. What seemed to be a random sculpture of a European explorer or writer appeared. However, with a little searching it became clear the statue was of Miguel de Cervantes, author of *Don Quixote*. The Spanish government gave the controversial gift to PKU: Don Quixote was a popular figure among early 20th-century Chinese intellectuals as he represented the struggle for spirituality, democracy and the self-reflexive intellectual; today students gather around the statue to debate the future of China (170). Not surprisingly the English website is different: There is no picture of the statue; instead the focus is on current relationships with the West. Most likely international students are not choosing China as a destination to learn about Don Quixote; however, the image might say to Chinese students and prospective faculty that this is a place where debate and discussion is encouraged.

PKU mentions its #1 ranking in a popular national ranking system. PKU does reference international rankings, but unlike Western universities, also acknowledges the high rankings of other Chinese universities and the pride Chinese should feel in this. On the Chinese website, PKU states it is #1 based on the China University Evaluation, but does not list the other popular ranking in China by the Chinese Academy of Management Science that places Peking in #2 ranking, and Tsinghua in #3.

Interestingly, both the PKU and Tsinghua Chinese websites include more information about QS and THE rankings than ARWU. Paradoxically, my research assistant, Yu Guo, discovered that, rather than telling prospective international students that Tsinghua is a highly ranked institution, the focus is on the university receiving graduate students from Harvard, MIT, Oxford and the University of Tokyo. Neither page focuses on world rankings to attract international students but on long history and reputation.

India

The origins of Indian universities and their relationship with their government is very different than in China. HEIs grew rapidly in India after independence in 1947. In 2014 there were 712 universities and 36,671 colleges (171, 172). Many colleges come under the national government's University Grants Commission (173). In 2013, the then Prime Minister of India noted that not one Indian university was in the top 200 in the THEWUR ranking, a comment that prompted a meeting that included the Planning Commission of India, the Ministry of Human Resources in India, THE, Thomson Reuters and the British Council. The participants are notable, particularly the British Council, with major interests in the international student market. The meeting attracted criticism, particularly from Indian academics. Nagaiah and Srimannarayana explain:

> The ranking methodology adopted is empirical in nature, question-able and not suitable for Indian universities, and is decided by cita-tions which may hold good for foreign universities to attract funds and international students. During the symposium, the absence of repre-sentatives from Indian universities was felt, while those representing THE and Thomson Reuters took centre stage, the issue of funding was raised by a handful of university representatives (174: p. 882).

Nagaiah and Srimannarayana go on to detail the lack of attention to Indian publications not captured by the Web of Science as well as to teaching and infrastructure. However, it appears the pressure to be a market for Western countries continues; for example, Narendra Modi, elected in 2014, promises to open up the education sector to foreign providers. A number of Western countries, including Canada, the UK and US, have issued briefs and held conferences to prepare HEIs to take advantage of the Foreign Provider Bill that allows foreign universities to set up programs in India.

The Indian government has promised greater funding for institutions capable of moving up in international rankings. India, like China, has encouraged mergers of institutions to concentrate financial resources in hopes of competing for world-class standing (175, 176). Also, like China, India has a high number of students that study abroad – over 189,000 in 2012 (176). Universities in India and China also receive many international students. The movement of students to and from China and India is not new. What has changed is that the movement of students is less tied to political and cultural alliances and more tied to economic trade.

The ARWU ranked the Indian Institute of Science (IISc) between 301 and 400. QS ranked the Indian Institute of Technology, Bombay (IITB) #222 and THE ranked it between 276–300. Interestingly neither is a comprehensive university, but both focus on male-dominated STEM fields. The IITB was set up with funds from UNESCO, and in 1961 it was decreed by Parliament to be an institute of national importance. A 2014 planning commission report pointed to continued issues with access to IITB, and noted that ninety-two percent of entrants to IITs are male, and stratification was based also on parents' education (177).

The Indian Institute of Science and Indian Institute of Technology

India has a number of national ranking systems; one of the more popular published by the weekly magazine *India Today* lists the Indian Institute of Science and the Indian Institute of Technology Bombay as the two top-ranked institutions in India, both of which are focused on science and technology. The IISc and the IITB have radically different websites.

The homepage in 2014 for IITB makes use of rotating images above the fold that express ideals such as: "Yearn to Endure" (images of people swimming) and "Yearn to Lead" (a man in a business suit on top of a large circular structure with blurred images of more men in suits a floor above him. The notion of enduring hard work to get to success is an important message that is twinned with images of power. To yearn refers to something that one longs for, that often has been lost; in this way IITB is inviting applicants to become part of finding what they long for. Here we see a strong focus on images that connect to material dimensions of jobs and money, as well as images that connect to good moral character. All the images are of men.

When I keyed in "ranking" in the search box for IITB, I found nothing, except on the prospective student page where the question "Why IITB?" is asked and the answer to the question is supplied: "IITB is the best technical school in the country and one of the top few globally." This one page includes all that HEI marketers suggest be covered: Town and Gown, lifestyle, prestige and career. Prospective applicants are told that faculty engage their students and that there is a strong alumni network. Alumni get good jobs. But most important:

> Some of the top reasons why students choose to be part of IITB is one that most people would least expect. While the academic curriculum forms a large part of the experience at IITB, the institute also offers a number of extracurricular activities.... .

The only context-specific information is in relation to Mumbai: "A green campus that is a welcome change from the concrete jungle that [is] the rest of Mumbai." The only image on this page is that of the IITB emblem. A green campus might signify environmental stewardship, but it might also be a spatial marker of Mumbai: The institute is not in the slums, not in the jungle, but in a separate physical space (178).

Conversely, the Indian Institute of Science tells the story of its founder as a way to ground current success. Readers are told IISc has "more than 2,000 active researchers working in almost all frontier areas of science and technology.... [and is] one of the oldest and finest centers of its kind in India, [with] a very high international standing in the academic world." This is the only site I examined that did not change much from the first time I looked at it in 2007 to 2014. There is reference to the university collaborating with Cambridge University Press in 2013 and images at the bottom with no text. The site is unlike the 12 other websites in that it appears low cost; its focus is mainly internal and giving prospective students information on how to apply to the IISc.

However, when I clicked on the webpage for the Office for International Relations, the color of the page became blue – similar to that of many Western universities – and images of four male students in casual dress and two women appear. A list is provided of 25 full-time international students on campus as of January 2014. Prospective students are told that the institute ranked 23rd in the Global Employability Survey, that is, "up 12 positions from the previous year's position of 35." They are also told IISc is the "best in the nation" and in some areas they are "ranked spectacularly well globally." The IISc and IITB sites were among the most interesting to analyze. The two sites are very different and the approach to rankings is subdued, particularly in comparison to the other websites included in this chapter.

South Africa

The South African HEI system consists of one coordinated system with 23 public universities, 50 vocational and technical colleges and a number of private institutions (178). South Africa is the only African country to have universities in the ARWU, QS and THEWUR and South Africa uses the ARWU for benchmarking (11). Inequities in South Africa between White institutions historically privileged through the apartheid era and historically Black universities continue, as do White enclaves (179). The first main policy objective listed in a 2013 government document entitled *White Paper for Post School Education and Training* is "education and social justice" and identifies lack of access in relation to gender, race and disability in the university sector as particularly problematic. The focus of the White Paper is on the need for universities to differentiate based on their strengths and on growing areas necessary for national development. The report also states South Africa is the most popular study destination for students in Africa; however, the discussion of internationalization is shorter and substantively different from that stated in Canadian, UK, USA or Indian policy documents and in translations of Chinese government documents. The White Paper states: "Internationalization should also be seen as an opportunity to take local and/or indigenous knowledge to the international community" (179). The focus is on sharing knowledge to solve problems such as HIV, sustainability and to "improve peace and co-operation" (3: p. 40). The White Paper does discuss the need for research, but is unusual in mentioning the importance of the humanities:

> A National Institute for Humanities and Social Sciences will be established to stimulate research and postgraduate studies in these vital disciplines. The DHET will provide support for the study and development of the African languages in our universities (179: p. xv).

The report also details the need for support of science, engineering and technology. Nowhere is improving South Africa's standing in university rankings mentioned.

The University of Cape Town (UCT) is ranked in the 201–300 category by ARWU and the University of Witwatersrand (Wits) in the 301–400 category. THEWUR ranks UCT #124; Wits is listed as between 251–275. QS gives UCT the rank of #141 and Wits #318. The number of Black students entering institutions such as UCT and Wits has grown dramatically; however, dropout rates remain high. Often students cannot continue to support themselves and their families through university (181).

Wits and University of Cape Town homepages

The UCT web design is similar to many sites examined; however, the website content is a departure from other sites in this study. There is a focus on the redress of the very recent apartheid past; for example, prominent on the webpage is a story about holding graduation ceremonies for those who did not attend during apartheid to protest the injustices of it. The site is very focused on context-specific images of people. With each image there is a story, with the majority focusing on inequity and protecting refugees. While the UCT homepage resembles other university websites – there are prominent links for donating, for admission and media links – there are also links to the Knowledge Co-op that invites the community to get involved in research projects aimed at community improvement. To the side of the Knowledge Co-op webpage are brochures on "The case against privatising knowledge." Open UCT also provides free access to theses, dissertations and other open educational resources. The university is clearly trying to grapple with South Africa's past – and the question of what it means to be a university in this context.

At the time of writing, 15 articles came up about rankings at UCT. Some were articles for news media. The focus of many of the pieces was UCT as the #1 institution in Africa and its continuing improvement in world rankings: "Most pleasing that the Times Higher Education (THE) Rankings placed UCT at number 107 in the world, the university's highest finish in any ranking yet." The use of headlines such as "NEW ERA AFOOT" focuses on progress and innovation in progress. However, UCT is also notable for its critique of rankings: Vice-Chancellor Max Price wrote an op-ed piece, published in a newspaper and posted on the UCT website, in which he emphasized the flaws in the rankings. He criticizes them for ignoring the need for resources to help students who have not received a high-quality K–12 education and the need to be socially responsive to marginalized communities. At least at the level of website rhetoric, UCT and Wits are open about structural disadvantage and the need for policies to mitigate disadvantage in ways other universities examined are not:

In European universities these resources could have been focused on research; at UCT they have to be diverted to academic development and social responsiveness programmes. This makes it all the more remarkable that we have made it to this position, but explains why there are very few developing-country universities in the top 200 (182).

There is pride expressed about being ranked, but caution that the rankings are problematic for developing countries and should not take away from the social mission of access and equity. There is also credit given to other African universities that do important work but are not as highly ranked because they do not do as much research. Nevertheless, Price concludes that rankings can't be ignored because they are used all over the world and prospective staff and students look at rankings to decide where to apply. Similar to Price's op-ed, all the articles on UCT's website that I captured expressed excitement about being ranked, albeit with some critique of the rankings.

In another headline, "UCT shines in World University Ranking by Subject," the verbal metaphor of light is paired with images of natural growth and strength. We see students walking towards or away from a Greco-Roman building, majestic Table Mountain behind. This article is also nuanced. The deputy vice-chancellor, Professor Daniel Visser, remarks, "As always, we are mindful that this is just one view of the cathedral, but we are very pleased about this renewed confirmation of our work" (183). The business school is closer in content and tone to the other websites; for example, it extols its superiority to other schools. However, even the business school provides a caution after extolling the value of its MBA – "Best-Value MBA Surges up International Ranking" – by noting that the rankings are only a tool and should not distract from a focus on Africa by trying to "reinvent Harvard" (184).

Unlike UCT, the focus of the Wits homepage is a large imposing Greco-Roman building along with small stories and images of a group of students. The top navigation bar is similar to other websites, except for the addition of a section called "Places and Spaces," which includes a virtual tour of the university. The most prominent image on the page is a building that links to tradition, but underneath the reader is told Wits is not only about tradition: "Wits Today – Changing Tomorrow." To the side, a story that deploys humor: "IG Nobel prize a pile of dung." It explains that "The Ig Nobel Prize honors achievements that make people LAUGH and then THINK." However, lest the reader think Wits is a joke, we are assured they are a world-class research institution, with top student athletes and experts able to comment on newsworthy issues.

Wits is open in employing the language of being "world class"; however, unlike institutions in the UK, US, and Canada, it contextualizes its status to Africa: "Wits is a world class research institute in Africa." In the UK and US, highly ranked institutions do not say "in North America" or "in Europe." Adam Habib, a nationally and internationally known scholar, became the vice-chancellor of Wits in 2013; in his inaugural address, Habib argues that South Africa needs to be competitive, but instead of focusing on university rankings, he turns to Finland, which does not have a university in the top 50, but scores in the top on human development indicators and argues that universities should all do research, but should nevertheless be differentiated in their educational mission. Habib stands out in his critical approach to rankings – especially when he argues that research-intensive universities should not receive more money just because they are more historically privileged than historically Black universities (185).

Nonetheless, Wits, as part of its strategic planning, sets itself the goal to be in the top 100 by 2020: "It has become a widely shared view that only world-class or leading universities can earn a rank in the top 500 league. Wits has repeatedly earned itself a good rank in this league of universities, asserting itself as one of the leading universities in the world" (186). Wits appears to have an active campaign to keep alumni involved. Alumni act as validators of the university's success, explaining that "Wits alumni have the edge in global rankings." Comparison to the West is frequent: "...the Center for World University Rankings (CWUR).... ranked Wits among the top 115 Universities in the world, with Harvard University at the number one spot" (July 17, 2014). What on the surface can seem like contradiction is perhaps a critical pragmatism: South Africa, given its recent past, seems much more sensitive to rankings as a technology of categorization that can further entrench inequity, and it seems to be at least rhetorically at the forefront of debate about education and equity. It is interesting to compare South Africa's approach to India's. India also has affirmative action programs, but concerns around equity are not present in the display of male wealth that is dominant throughout the IITB site.

UCT and Wits have ambivalent attitudes toward rankings: Both use media and public addresses to point to the need for government to better fund education, but both also point to ranking bias that favors wealthy nations. Now we turn to one of the countries most associated with international rankings.

The United Kingdom

The Times Higher Education Rankings comes out of the UK, a leader in using rankings for resource-allocation decision-making in government and universities. Thatcher is widely recognized for introducing the mass privatization of public services, accompanied by an intensive audit culture; her administration also abolished tenure in HEIs through redundancies and made dramatic changes in labor relations (187). Funding became tied to performance of individual faculty members, and departments were ranked. While Oxford and Cambridge were not dramatically impacted by these changes as much as other UK universities, it is interesting to analyze the continuities and changes evident in two of the highest-ranked institutions in the world. While there have been a number of reports on higher education in the UK, the most relevant to examining the role of rankings is the 2011 White Paper, which deregulated higher education to allow for-profit education and a substantial increase in tuition fees (188) and generated much controversy, including "In Defence of Public Higher Education," a response launched in *The Guardian* that was endorsed by hundreds of academics and academic associations (189).

The UK's Cambridge and Oxford consistently are ranked in the top 10 institutions worldwide. In 2013, for example, QS ranked the University of Cambridge #2, ARWU gave the same university a #5 ranking, and the Times Higher Education ranked Oxford #3.

Oxford and Cambridge

Oxford's website in 2014 has high-quality images and catchy headlines. The bottom of the page has the link, "THIS IS OXFORD – LATEST NEWS & FEATURES." The sound/image bites are paired with images of stability: For example, in December, an image of a Christmas tree in front of an old building and in large letters, "OVER 900 FULLY-FUNDED GRADUATE SCHOLARSHIPS AVAILABLE." Under this are three images and stories of high media interest: one about personal breathalyzers; another foregrounding a Chinese girl with an old truck behind her, "Why reform of China's one-child policy has had little effect in boosting fertility levels." The focus is entrepreneurial: research, attracting international students, the wealth of the institution and its reputation.

A number of stories on the Oxford and Cambridge homepages are written as news stories similar in style to stories found in mainstream media; for example, stories about the Global South show desperate people dealing with tragedy. People with medical masks are shown carrying coffins, with the headline "IMF Lending Undetermined Healthcare Provision in Ebola-stricken West Africa." The Global South is presented as the beneficiary of the Global North. Another headline explains that "Technology developed at the University of Cambridge lies at the heart of a commercial process that can turn toothpaste tubes and drink pouches into both aluminium and fuel in just three minutes." Here research also connects to the hot-button topic of sustainability.

Both universities refer to rankings that affirm their status. For example, Dr. Wendy Pratt, Director of the Russell Group of Universities, said, "These figures provide another indication that UK universities punch well above their weight on the world stage, with Russell Group Institutions[2] (190) taking four of the top seven spots including Cambridge at number one. We have better universities than any other country, apart from the US" (September 5, 2011). Oxford is cheekier in reporting ranking: "Oxford ranked best in Europe in World Rankings for Computer Science (again)." The "again" denotes a certainty they would be confirmed and almost a boredom with being proven right once more.

"Why Oxford?" connects Oxford to its long tradition of academic excellence and positions it to continue this leadership. Readers are told, "The University's international reputation for world-leading research and resources, combined with a beautiful city alive with activity, attracts students from all over the world." Under this text is an image of two young women in lab coats leaning over microscopes with the tab, "Research and Teaching"; adjacent is an image of a modern glass building with the subheading "Ranking" which leads the reader to more examples of Oxford's excellence, "Consistently ranked as one of the top universities in the world"; finally, there is an image of an old building and blue sky with the text, "Extensive Support to Help You Achieve your Potential." Oxford's two-minute video animation of its year in review starts with, "The best part of being 1000 years old is still being in great shape according to the Research Exercise Framework – and that is across the spectrum." The focus of the video is showing selected research contributions to the public good; for example, viewers are told Oxford scientists created technology to help the blind and researchers assist the poor.

The audience is also informed that Oxford is the place where discoveries about spiders and music, climate change and finding a cure for Ebola are made. Such research does not go unnoticed: Oxford scientists receive many awards, including top honors given by the Queen. In under two minutes, the video refers to both global to local research, a storyline that confirms Oxford as an institution of enormous importance at both macro and micro levels. Next we look at the US, known for its dominance in international rankings.

The USA

As Hazelkorn argues, "The United States presents a more complicated picture because of its federal system, but individual states vie with each other over the status of their 'flagships'" (191: p. 20), a contest complicated by a complex network of both public and private HEIs. Public universities supplement state and federal government revenue with tuition fees, fundraising and private research funds. Rankings are used to compete within the US, and international rankings are used by some states to assess their system.

The federal government provides an important revenue stream through special purpose funds that are generally accompanied by substantial compliance requirements (192) and in 2014, President Obama announced that his administration would develop a rating system that would give HEIs a score based on indicators. The private HE sector, in particular, was sharply opposed to the plan, but so too was some of the public sector. An article in *The New York Times* states that Obama's argument is that the federal government provides over $150 billion a year in federal loans and grants to HEIs, yet tuition continues to rise while graduation rates fall. The article provides examples of some of the increasingly lavish amenities at universities that marketers suggest HEIs create to increase application numbers, an added cost that makes it more difficult for lower- and middle-income people to attend. In response, a federal rating system would see universities allocated funds based on indicators such as financial aid policies, job outcomes after graduation, affordability and accessibility (193). Obama's plan and media coverage around it captures the contested space of who and what is responsible for HEI choices in the US.

In 2014, QS ranked MIT as the Top University in the World, ARWU declared Harvard to be #2 in the world, and the Times Higher Education ranked Caltech as the #1 university in the world.

Caltech, MIT and Harvard homepages

On the Caltech website homepage, there are 29 thumbnail sized images of people including young-looking scientists as well as images representing various areas of science; the visuals provide a sense of stability and tradition alongside the colorful pictures of young faculty and students. Unlike universities in India, China and South Africa that focus on being the best in the country or continent, Caltech's coverage of rankings, similar to MIT and Harvard, focuses on being globally superior, not just in the USA: "Caltech Again Named World's Top University in *Times Higher Education* Global Ranking." Another release from the graduate student office gives a number of rankings with an image of a welcoming, modern sitting area.

Perhaps the most interesting Harvard piece on rankings is found under "Quick Facts," which explains that rankings don't measure everything and to be careful to know who is doing the ranking. However, the article then goes on to "SELECT RANKINGS," all of which point to Harvard being at or close to the top. The focus is on STEM rankings, and the list ends with a table of the occupations of recent Harvard graduates; the future certainly looks promising for those who make the choice to go to Harvard.

On the MIT homepage are images of prehistoric gazelle, and plants on a plate with what appears to be a prototype of an early fork and knife. The accompanying story is about the diet of Neanderthals. I was unable to locate evidence that Neanderthals used forks, knives and plates, but the image artfully blends the old of Neanderthals and the new of apparent refinement and civilization. The main navigation bar includes Admission, Discover, Apply, Afford, Visit, Follow and My MIT, but what stands out is the use of humor. To the side, animated faces with articles by students: "Skipping class and failing bio – A practical guide to poor life choices" or "A White Christmas Escaping Boston to go to more snow." There are students in lab coats and stories not about science – but describing the lifestyle provided by MIT.

I found 16 articles about rankings; 14 out of the 16 show the same image of what looks like a traditional academic quad area. "2014 Rankings: MIT Sits at the Top" opens with:

> Aside from the first day of classes, no event signifies the start of another academic year better than the U.S. News and World Report's annual rankings of the United States' best colleges and universities. And similar to past years, MIT finds itself at or near the top in nearly every category.

The article goes on to say MIT is also ranked highly in QS and Forbes. One interesting link is to "The strangest ranking? A recent photo gallery from CNBC that lists MIT as the sixth-best university for billionaire alumni." The link leads to a picture of well-known Republican Party supporter David Koch with a hard hat on. On the same MIT webpage viewers are invited to "Share your thoughts on the latest wave of rankings in the comments below, or on Facebook and Twitter" and hyperlinks are provided for Facebook, Twitter and ranking sites mentioned in the article. By sharing thoughts, MIT alumni can reinforce the excellence of the brand and provide MIT data as to how members of their marketing universe feel about the rankings. Here we see a full acceptance of the USNWR as legitimate; the language is promotional and sometimes draws on humor, e.g., MIT's ranking as "sixth-best university for billionaire alumni." The message is you too can be wealthy if you graduate from MIT.

My first impression was that the MIT, Harvard and Caltech sites had substantially different approaches: Caltech's homepage looks like a photo gallery, Harvard's is more text-heavy but with a prominent video and MIT has just one image, but with access to a photo gallery. However, upon closer analysis, it became clear that all use promotional language aimed at increasing the number of student applications, international students and donations to the institutions. All three institutions use different rankings to show they are #1: For example, if a department is #1 in a particular ranking, that becomes the focus. In all three institutions, we can see logics that comply with rankings (for example, showing that the institution has a high percentage of international faculty or substantial research dollars).

Harvard, MIT and Caltech are not wanting for students but the competition for being the most selective university is fierce. Indeed, it is to the institution's benefit to have many students apply to show that increasing numbers are rejected. Homepages for MIT, Harvard and Caltech represent diversity mainly through Black and Latino faces and bodies; curiously, diversity is sometimes represented as a discrete category; for example, the MIT site, under initiatives, lists "energy| cancer| diversity| global."

Conclusion

Websites could be seen as a sort of semiotic parade: Symbols are displayed in different combinations with hopes of attracting new consumers and retaining existing ones. Symbols are different in different contexts: The UK and US use symbols and language that assume the audience knows they are world class and can afford to appear bored to be at the top of the rankings once again and use humor to report results; South Africa, on the other hand, draws on recent memories of apartheid to represent universities as part of the community and as participants in national struggles for equity and justice.

Like Askehave (194), who discovered the increasing presence of promotional texts and what she called "mood types" on websites in Finland, Scotland, Australia and Japan, I found many images of happy students and faculty on university homepages. Images of nature are prominent, as is data showing that students are socially fulfilled, "happy customers." Academics are given lower profile: Indeed, like Ng (83), I found that academic study and hard work is downplayed and a fun, beautiful lifestyle is highlighted.

There are commonalities across the websites I analyze in this chapter that point to what Fairclough calls "naturalized common sense" (195), based on relations of power that create the context of knowledge as commodity. The most prevalent metaphors are around a race to the top, rising and falling, growth and competition. Textual metaphors of rising in the ranks are sometimes paired with visual metaphors of growth, such as mountains and trees or images of iconic figures such as Einstein.

The Chinese versions of the PKU and Tsinghua sites draw on the language of nation building and progress, as do the Indian sites. Conversely, Canada, the US, and UK focus on individuals achieving personal wealth and fulfillment. Here we see that websites are not created in a vacuum, but part of the larger cultural politics and relationships between government and universities; increasingly, particularly in Canada, the US and UK, the relationship of universities to the promotion of capitalism is overt.

I found the inverse of what I expected in terms of diversity within and across websites. Canada has a decentralized higher education system that is governed by provincial, territorial and local governments; government does not have a formal say in the day-to-day operating of the university. Similarly, US and UK universities are represented as autonomous. Chinese and Indian universities, on the other hand, are governed by their respective national governments. Nevertheless, the greatest diversity in websites was found in China and India, with the greatest level of isomorphism (convergence) in Canada, the US and UK.

The type of images, color schemes and navigation bars were remarkably similar, as was the content.

Visual and verbal metaphors are often understood as context-specific and open to many interpretations (196); however, visual and verbal metaphors – of being "world class," crown, podium, innovation, entrepreneurship and happiness – cross most of the contexts I analyzed. The verbal and visual language of connecting education to private economic gain crosses national and cultural boundaries. There were many references on all the sites to distinction, but there were differences, particularly evident throughout the UCT website in South Africa. Graphical representations including reproductions of tables and graphs from rankers that show superiority are common, particularly in Canadian, US, and UK universities in the sample. Further, all countries in the sample talk about their top placement in their country or, in the case of South Africa, on the continent; The US, UK, and Canada, however, speak more about their status as top institutions in the world. This shows a similar visual language emerging that encompasses the discourse of education as that which can be measured and therefore compared or ranked against other educational products.

Absences

Understanding how a university brands itself requires looking not just at how it presents itself, but what is invisible through normative relationships of power: Rankings "measure what is measurable in quantities that signal quality; what they exclude appears to have less value" (197: p. 1). The normative relationship of the Global North helping the Global South was apparent as was evidence of "technologies of differentiation separating Us from Them" (198: p.370). Race is, of course, a social construct, but one that is very powerful: Images of Black people were usually used to signal beneficiaries of White science and teaching and White continues to be represented as normative in Western universities (198).

The findings of my analysis of the UK, US, and Canada are similar to those of Kem Saichaie's 2011 study: "Of the 453 images in the study, 98 feature a non-white actor (21%) and 146 feature a female actor (32%)" (158: p. 2). In Canada, the US and UK, leadership was predominately represented as white and male; in South Africa, China and India, images of leadership were predominately male. I found an absence of markers of disability and gender identity.

Smoothing over the contradictions

Sihua writes: "The brands of international education that are being imagined, constructed, and desired are unevenly weighted in favour of the economic imperative, academic instrumentalism, and a kind of study tourism" (199: p. 36). Ranking creates a dilemma for universities evident in my analysis of the websites. The universities in this sample are under pressure to attain and maintain world-class status as each university and each country competes for its slice of the global knowledge economy. Paradoxically, universities that form alliances with other national institutions – e.g., industry or government – to compete globally risk the loss of substantive autonomy, but remaining independent risks invisibility, revenue loss and irrelevancy.

Overall high-ranking universities conform to representing who they are in ways consistent with what is deemed excellence by major rankers. The visual manifestation of this effort becomes evident in analyzing website layout, design and images: There is substantial conformity to the recommendations of the burgeoning branding literature aimed at HEIs to emphasize lifestyle for product differentiation, as well as on the natural beauty or urban amenities offered by a university. Rankings were naturalized: With the exception of South Africa, rankings were reported as useful facts on university websites. Occasionally there was a qualifier or caution to be careful about what rankings one used, but all institutions seemed to believe that rankings were unavoidable and many used rankings to pressure government to provide increased funding.

There is evidence of the emergence of a global visual education language consistent with global higher educational governance. The university websites I analyzed fabricate a narrative of coherence and consensus: The dominant theme in university websites constructs the university as place of enlightenment and neutral numbers representing the truth to prospective students, allowing them to choose their personal educational journeys. Images and text tap into powerful emotions around success, responsibility and autonomy.

Nonetheless, there can never really be consensus on what counts as an excellent higher education; indeed, if there was consensus, the purpose of the university would cease to exist. Naidoo, drawing on Bourdieu, reminds us that a "field is not a product of consensus but the dynamic product of permanent conflict" (200: p. 1146). In this chapter and the next chapter, thinking about field is helpful for understanding "a relational approach which focuses on interactive processes between and within universities" (200: p. 1146). By looking at internal and external relations simultaneously, we can see how individuals use their capital in a field and how institutions position themselves and are positioned within the branded and ranked education field.

6
Boundary Workers: University Public Affairs Workers

University public affairs offices at universities play the central role in determining the stories a university tells to itself and the outside world. These stories include what research and knowledge is most prized and who produces it, what activities happen at the universities and who participates. Universities tell their stories through legacy media, websites, social media, media releases, Facebook, YouTube, podcasts, and a plethora of other venues and use both earned media (stories they pitch and get media to cover) and paid media (advertising the university pays for). It is difficult to get exact figures for how much Canadian universities spend on marketing, branding, public affairs, and specific efforts to improve reputation rankings. Budget lines for student services, for example, can also include money for marketing as part of student recruitment.

Some universities integrate public affairs, media, government, external relations, alumni relations and development in one office; others have both central communications offices and communications units in faculties, departments and schools. In common, however, is a substantial increase in funds devoted to promoting the university over the last 10 years. Bolan and Robertson show a dramatic increase in spending on public affairs at Canadian universities; they found, for example, that the communications budget for Windsor went from $622,000 in 2002–2003 to $1,200,000 in 2007–2008 and the budget at Western went from $913,230 in 2000–2001 to $2,265,352 in 2010–2011 (44). These figures suggest that communications and marketing have dramatically increased in importance; ironically, however, there are few studies that examine how universities promote themselves and what this means for the ways universities tell and act on the stories they want to tell.

Indeed, while we know there is an increased focus on public relations, we do not know who makes the decisions about what to say about a university. In this chapter, I analyze interviews with eight senior public affairs staff from seven universities. In some universities, they are called communications directors and in others they are executive directors or vice-presidents; all have had years of experience in communications, some in media, others in government or business. I committed to all participants that I would not identify them or the institutions they work for, and for this reason I use Participant 1 etc. to identity them. (See Appendix 1 for methodological information.)

The interviews focused on the decision-making process of senior PA workers from Tier 1 research-intensive universities across Canada. Questions included: What and who influences decision-making around stories about academic work, including what should be told (and not told)? Who are the audiences for various communications and why? How do senior PA workers perceive social diversity and equity issues in relation to branding and institutional reputation? How do they negotiate contested views among academics and university administration about what the university should stand for? And finally, how do they exercise agency in diverse and competitive contexts?

Public affairs as boundary work

In this chapter I approach PA personnel as boundary workers. Boundary workers work between industry and academics, government and academics, and media and academics. I draw on the work of Fisher and Atkinson-Grosjean who looked at industry liaison officers (74); they describe the role of industry liaison officers as doing "boundary work" in their role of commercializing academic research. For example, public relations staff do boundary work in branding universities: Like industry liaison officers, public affairs personnel are expected to translate and to increase "boundary permeability," and one can argue their attempts have been largely successful. Prior to the 1990s, for example, "marketing was viewed as undignified, even vulgar; university officials thought that students would suffer if recruitment practices went beyond a straight-and-narrow informational approach" (44: p. 567). However, today universities have virtual tours and swag to give away at recruitment fairs along with raffles for iPads.

Boundary permeability and the emergence of boundary worker roles developed in federal and provincial policy contexts in Canada alongside an increased emphasis on rankings. Boundaries have become more permeable based on new requirements for grant funding and the need for universities to raise funds in response to public cuts. Canadian government policies have blurred boundaries between academic autonomy and basic research versus "industrially relevant" research (200: p. 3): Funding for research has increasingly become contingent on connections to industry.

Rankings have also become standard points of measurement for the effectiveness of public affairs. The work of PA offices is a form of political labor that involves workers having to figure out what can be said and done in different contexts. For example, PA officers, as I later describe, often talk to academics differently from how they address media or government. I do not propose the work of these people is the same in all contexts; however, we can see some convergence in the discourses used among senior public affairs staff interviewed for this study. While the focus of this chapter is on Canada, the boundary between public affairs and disciplinary work emerges as significant frontier to be negotiated in other contexts, as well. For instance, Sidhu, who interviewed marketing personnel in the UK and Australia, explains:

> I was struck by the extent to which academics had either been edged out or had removed themselves from key strategic decisions about international education. Responses like this one were not uncommon from marketing personnel: "Academics get upset. But then you don't ask academics" (199: p. 37).

Within a highly competitive marketplace, questions related to a university's visibility are central to maintaining or expanding market share. Public affairs offices must communicate to media, policymakers, prospective students and their parents, alumni, industry, various communities, potential donors, academics and the wider public. They must negotiate their own position among and within these different groups and fields to ensure maximum visibility of their institutions, an effort that is often viewed by faculty as a threat to academic autonomy and yet another sign of the corporatization of universities.

Rankings are associated with branding, reputation management and greater government and industry funding. All participants spoke about the increased interest and attention paid to rankings and competition by senior leadership at their university:

> We need more than a guy in a room filling out the all forms and sending them in.... That's not a strategy for managing our rankings..., so now

we actually have a COMs [communications] person who is proactively tracking this, working with the rankings group, so it's all mapped out on the calendar .... We've got to have someone assigned to get the information, assess the information for every major ranking. We have a briefing note sent over incredibly quickly ... [to] our executive leadership team that says here's the results and here's the communications recommendation.... Sometimes we say we're not going to say anything about this. If asked, this is what we'll say, and in some cases we say we want to share this with our own community and in some cases, we say this is like a huge deal, so we're going to be proactive with the media (Participant 9).

Participant 9 is explaining how the job of public affairs isn't just about filling out forms, but imagining various courses of action. Doing such work requires research: Public affairs officers need someone to find the needed information, then analyze and prepare that information in a format accessible to university leadership and that allows them to make good decisions. Communications staff are involved in intensive negotiations and Participant 9's description of the work compares to that of choreographers: Successful PA workers must shape coherent stories that appeal to diverse and sometimes antagonistic audiences (or at least make them politically palatable and newsworthy). Such choreography requires a great deal of preparation. Think of plays or ballets that seem to just naturally flow and the hundreds of hours of work – visible only to those behind the scenes – required to create seamless performances. Similarly, news stories about a university do not just appear, but they require the efforts of public affairs workers to pitch stories to appropriate media and to frame stories in ways that are coherent with the performance of the brand.

Framing a story is a distinguishing feature of public affairs work and involves determining key messages and their priority, activities somewhat foreign in the culture of universities: Communications work is largely simplifying issues, e.g., looking for the hook, the headline, while much academic work involves looking for contradiction, nuance and limitation. The essence of strategic communications is to create a narrative that identifies an institution's niche within a competitive market. Media coverage then becomes leverage and an echo chamber; if the excellence of an institution is repeated enough times by what appears to be external validators, the chance of commercial success is enhanced.

Reputational excellence is, of course, a key feature of ranking. Participants spoke about pumping out positive rankings especially to international media and at student recruitment fairs (Participant 1) and reputation surveys were mentioned as important by a number of participants. Participant 8 makes clear why the surveys are important: "Performing or optimizing your performance on your reputation surveys [is crucial] because two of the big rankings have a big chunk of it driven by reputation surveys." Participants emphasized the importance of rankings, but also mentioned not really knowing how to improve rankings:

> We're trying to get a good understanding of what the rankings are, what they mean. We know it's important to our prospects. And how do we look at them here? We can't get a straight answer on how to deal with them and what it means. And we've been trying for a couple of years now just to get an overall ranking strategy (Participant 7).

Participants do not take rankings at face value; they attempt to decode and reconstruct them and use them to corner a niche in a competitive marketplace. Again we see the boundary work of trying to figure out rankings within the larger context of branding of universities. Participants explained that communication strategies were based in a university's position in relation to other HEIs: A university ranked near the top by the "Big Three" generally focused on these rankings whereas other universities stressed subject-specific rankings or student satisfaction surveys.

While participants spoke about the importance of institutional vision, many did so by employing the same language of indicators used by the "Big Three" rankers: Goals included increasing citations, attracting international students and investments, and making amenities attractive to prospective students. Some, however, included such considerations as community engagement. Rankings, however, were not seen as ends in themselves, but tools for other ends; for example, cuts in funding were mentioned as requiring more aggressive branding to improve rankings in order to attract high-fee-paying international students. Goals are contested, and the role of PA workers is to negotiate these contradictions.

Branding and reputation

Participants spoke about the importance of branding in developing connections with industry as well as in student recruitment. They often used corporate language, such as positioning the university brand, optimizing performance, core priorities, and signature areas. All spoke about the increased attention senior university leaders place on branding:

> There has been a recognition in the last couple of years, amongst top university officials, that it matters that we are consistent in our brand, ... [and] that we need to do more marketing in markets where we want to attract students and faculty. ... We want a central message out there about the excellence of ... X University and ... [it] could be around an incredible ranking that we get internationally. We're going to place those ads in places where we think it's going to matter (Participant 1).

Participant 1 points out how branding employs certain common communication features: For example, the language of community is frequent and often used to capture prospective high-value students and donors while the first person plural underlines the university as community. The importance of a coherent message was evident throughout my interviews and was usually connected to acquiring top international students and faculty and funding from government, industry and alumni. Indeed, the notion of a unified brand impacted all communications activities: Rankings exert pressure for one message that emphasizes exceptionality and selectivity. Branding, participants pointed out, is not just about letterhead, but goes "right down to the facilities trucks driving around here on campus" (Participant 11).

The participants were also very much aware of the contested nature of their discourse and were careful about the language they used with different audiences.

> We don't actually call it branding here because it upsets academics. It's too Bay Street.[1] It's too Wall Street. It's too business. And I can have a beer and talk about how ridiculous that is. But it's the reality here. So what we did is we produced a promise. Right? So we, we have a promise ... (Participant 4).

Participant 4 explained that the language of promise was used so as not to anger academics who found talk of "branding" offensive. Here we see an example of being caught between corporate media language and academic discourse; academics, from this PA worker's perspective, sometimes appear overly emotional and in need of special handling. We also see difference in language for different audiences: Within private circles, "branding" can be used. However, all participants were aware of sensitivities around branding and that they employ contested discourses that are often viewed with suspicion. Some participants saw the tension between PA and academia as a matter of misunderstanding on the part of academics.

Some participants explained how there were so many desired objectives in some university plans that it was impossible to have a consistent brand. However, Participant 4 spoke about some senior leaders who were on the "MBA plan" whereas others spoke about the importance of branding in their university's strategic plan:

> And so we have a very strong strategy. We've brand-built an academic plan and a research plan underneath that. So those are our road maps for how we're going to get there (Participant 9).

Here there is a plan and strategy, and it seems clear-cut: Everything is encompassed in the brand. What research is highlighted and who is highlighted are part of the brand strategy. First comes strategy, and underneath, the academic plan and research plan. Absent is who is left out when there is one plan for an institution that offers humanities, STEM and social sciences, and claims to welcome a plurality of ways of knowing. Nuances, doubts and lack of certainty are absent, while strategy and messages attempt to convey military precision.

> We are all involved in branding. We are all...champions of our university and I think that what the main area that research communications intersects with the branding is that we aim to be one of the most distinguished universities in Canada in XXX main signature areas (Participant 3).

To be distinguished is linked with having focused "signature" areas that allow the telling of a consistent story that all members can champion. Some universities spoke more in terms of international competition, and others spoke about provincial competition to gain greater government and business support. "We" will be recognized. What happens to those not recognized? To those not part of the signature? Or who think the signature is meaningless? This becomes a question of recognition: What is recognized as "signature?" Who decides? On what basis? Who is excluded?

Developing a singular brand requires some form of consensus – a special challenge in universities. Overlapping discourses involving different members of an enormously diverse university community make dialogue a challenge and consensus unlikely at best. Yet, the stakes are high for PR workers: If they don't get a coherent plan through, they can't do their work. And even if they have a plan and a coherent brand, there is no guarantee that it will be supported by all members of the university community. Branding is now expressed at both the institutional level and that of the individual academic or employee:

> We also live in an era of personal brand and people are taking more responsibility for how they present themselves and are eager to present themselves. When I started in media relations at the university, there would be people who were willing to talk to media – although sometimes they looked at that as a real interference to their day. There were very few people who were, ah, viewed it as an opportunity (Participant 2).

Voluntary mobilization to support one's brand – and the university's – is viewed by public affairs officers as linked to being responsible: A good academic embodies his/her institution. Here we begin to see the management of subjectivities: What is a good academic and what are the expectations of an academic to promote the university brand? People's individual reputation becomes their brand. Maintaining the high ranking of an institution becomes important to one's own sense of worth. Jürgen Habermas might see this as an example of the colonization of lifeworld (202). The lifeworld of academia is colonized by the systems world of branding and so people begin to see their own success as determined by their ability to align or realign themselves with the brand of the institution.

However, not all academics are viewed as "responsible." Participant 3 talked about two researchers with opposing views that are expressed through media:

> I think that this is not good for our brand because I think it looks like we don't have a balanced approach at our university, that we're out of step with what the leading scientific community is thinking ... Because the problem is these two people, they, they love to brand themselves. They're both in op-eds and they write letters to the editor. And I had a media person recently say to me, "Do you realize what this is doing to your reputation?" (Participant 3).

Here academics become liabilities: They are outside "our brand." The use of "our" is frequent in the interviews. Getting academics to buy into the brand requires that they recast their daily routines to include brand work such as contacting media with the right brand messages, recruiting high-value international students and publishing in journals that will increase brand visibility. It seems clear here that boundary work takes place at many levels – from the personal to the career boundaries within HEI. Moreover, the realm of public affairs in universities is discursively and practically located on two contradictory normative trajectories; working with academics "out of step" with the brand involves getting them to support the brand, but the core of scholarship is disagreement, debate and the sanctity of "academic freedom." The risks of damaging the brand are material: losing private funds in a marketized environment where reputation from a corporate worldview is everything.

Communications work is not only about branding within the university community, but connecting with various external communities. Boundary work crosses many borders, and so reputation and brand management becomes linked to "issues management", and common issues management events included suicides, sexual assaults and social media bullying. One participant talked about how senior management started to see the importance of communications after "suicides of students that created... management and reputation management issues... [that] really kind of escalated the changing of what it is we do." Issues management emphasizes communicating to stakeholders, particularly parents and alumni, what the institution is doing:

> The recommendation from the communications front is: Look, we want to be seen as a leader in sort of moving the needle on policies around this stuff and programs and supports. Like we have good stories to tell there, so let's not shy away from it, even if we don't have all the answers right now, very few universities do (Participant 11).

The notion of "front" brings to mind the language of a battlefield. We need to pick good stories to compete in the arms race for students. Public affairs offices are expected to make quick decisions as issues of the day and crises unfold, which explains the tension sometimes felt between public affairs and academics. Academics, in contrast, lose capital if they make snap decisions about research and are caught out for being sloppy or, worse, fraudulent. Issues management has become an issue when academic research might upset funders. All participants stated that academic freedom is protected, but that government or industry might be given a "heads-up" when findings that could be upsetting to them were released: "We give heads up to government and central administration that a story may hit where one of our academics is saying bad things about our key stakeholder, you know, the people that give us all the money" (Participant 1). Again, public affairs workers are in a buffer zone, responsible for protecting the interest of funders while preserving at least the appearance of autonomy.

Criticism of the university as a whole often leads to another type of issue management in which public affairs workers, even though employed by university, become mediators between government/ industry and the university. The complexity of boundary work, of managing subjectivities, is evident in this example: His job is to maintain the brand of the institution by facilitating an academic's media engagement while also being sensitive to academic autonomy. Ultimately, he must protect the institution's major revenue streams and therefore he informs government and industry of potential embarrassments. Clearly, one important feature of branding aims at aligning the social and academic and, if in misalignment, then strategies must be created to mitigate damage, also known as "issues management." All participants also described another critical (and related) alignment challenge for branding: Telling the story of the university.

Strategic planning

Strategic planning was very tightly connected to reputation management. Many participants spoke about shifting from releasing stories about academics doing research to finding stories that would advance the institution's brand:

> On the side of the journalists coming and asking for someone to comment on X or Y, like really, most of that commentary stuff, a lot of it, probably 80% of it, doesn't do anything to further the university's reputation either. Like having Joe Blow Professor of Political Science at XX in a news story about XXX [well-known Canadian politician], or whatever, isn't really helping us raise our reputation as an innovator (Participant 11).

Here is an example of the boundary work between PA and journalists; journalists are not merely served by the public affairs staff, but PA directs what stories are useful. Strategic planning is connected to reputation management and many participants spoke about shifting from releasing stories about academics doing research to finding stories that would advance the institution's brand.

They also spoke about the number of media stories as no longer an adequate measure or success. Researchers talking about their findings without a focus on how a world-class institution enabled their work were seen as a waste of time:

> We got 15 media hits today. Isn't that great? Well, no.... None of them talked about the institution, none of the researcher quotations said, not in these words but this, this, this essence – none of them said "We couldn't have done it without the University of X because it's the greatest research institution in the country" (Participant 4).

Participant 4 is explaining that just having a professor talk about her/his research is not a worthwhile media hit: A good media hit is one with a member of the university speaking about themselves as productive, happy members of the brand and spreading the brand's reputation through testimonials to its life-changing properties. In consequence, media metrics thus become a form of assessment of branding: Participant 4 elaborated on his frustration with media stories (hits) that did not mention the university and therefore did nothing to change the perception of the university based on the strategic communication strategy. What is needed is glorifying the university. It is not only about changing what journalists write about, but how they write, that is, the framing of the story.

Success of a university's strategic plan is now often measured by the reaction of the "core audience," which, in turn, is the target of the branding activities. Many participants were clear on the difference between communications in general (e.g., responding to journalists' request to find an academic on the topic du jour) and strategic communications:

> [At] the end of the year, what do we want our core audiences to think of this institution? Or at the end of five years, how will we have changed perceptions about this institution? We have a strategic plan that's very clearly articulated, and there are areas where we believe that the University of X will be a world leader. So it's building that reputation, building that profile of the institution and the researcher (Participant 8).

Perception, that is, building an image, is therefore crucial. The branding goal is that when someone hears the name of University X, world-class status will come to mind. The language of positioning the university brand and optimizing performance was common in my interviews.

Some universities spoke more in terms of international competition, and others talked about challenging provincial competition to gain greater government and business support. Participants described the importance of being seen as "value added" to government and industry.

> We're constantly feeding the government, the provincial government in particular, and in some cases the federal government which provides research funding. We feed them stories and/or provide them with links and they've been known to repurpose them in their international travels as well and international efforts (Participant 1).

The use of the language of "repurposing" was common: Universities are not just competing for government funding, but for government to privilege stories from their institution when on international trade missions and thereby contribute to the branding exercise – yet another example of the boundary work.

Inclusion and exclusion

We see that boundary work involves negotiating the relationship between the global and local. High rankings were connected to being able to attract the best students and faculty. The participants reported working closely with offices associated with internationalizing and with translating materials that highlighted ranking for high priority areas – in particular, China, India and Brazil. They mentioned two motivations: "The emphasis on that has grown because international students not only increase the potential of bringing in the best and the brightest from around the world, that's rhetoric, but it also brings in more revenue" (Participant 4). Again participants are aware of conflicting discourses, but only one is public: Stating that international students were sought after for revenue would be contradictory to the positioning of an institution as world class and, therefore, highly selective.

When I asked about underrepresented fields and demographics, the response was more varied. Many participants said that they had not really thought about the demographic of stories they pitched or posted on internal university media; others explained that they considered the demographics of academics on a regular basis: "We're conscious of it and we talk about it. But having said that, I'm not shy to say that it is not a focused enough concern.... The institution is not that serious about that" (Participant 4). I asked participants what their estimate would be for the number of women and men, indigenous people, people of color and people with disabilities on their university websites and in pitches made to external media, and in what roles. Participant 8 explained that when planning to take images for university materials they had not planned for images of people using a wheelchair, but:

> We do have one individual in a wheelchair, [who] was someone who visited the campus – that kind of thing. Like we hadn't almost planned the wheelchair participant, but then we spoke to our diversity officer, they commented on the fact that this individual was included (Participant 8).

The focus is on images of diversity, but this does not mean there is actual diversity: In the example above, what was important was to show someone in a wheelchair and that image demonstrated a diverse university community. Many participants said they liked the question and that it caused them to think:

> I don't even know that I could provide an estimate to be honest. I'd maybe have to give that some thought or go back and check because I've never actually thought of it that way. I've never thought in terms of whether it's male or female, uh, except on very, very small items. Like if you're talking about a woman's issue, it's nice to have a woman researcher, right? (Participant 3)

Women or minorities are pulled out to talk about issues that are seen as impacting them rather than when they have unique and valuable knowledge. Stories that are promoted need to fit with the branding and strategic plan of the universities, that is, the "core" or "signature" areas.

Other participants responded that their concern was who was best to promote the university brand regardless of equity. They spoke about women being less likely to self-promote or to talk to media, and attributed this reluctance to concerns for work-life balance. Participant 1 explained:

> So we've had women come back to us and say, "I'd love to do that but I have to be home at 5:30 every night to, to get my daughter from

day-care." And we don't run into that with males as much. There's no doubt about that.

Participant 1 spoke about not seeing the lack of women in media as a gender issue, but more as a cultural reticence to talk to media. She said that she tried to encourage academics to speak with media and explained to them that talking to media was a way to market themselves and their research, which could lead to greater funding and, at no cost, getting the word out about their research. None of the participants mentioned any reluctance of scholars to fit their work into branded messages or quick sound bites.

Some participants saw some groups as less willing to engage with media. Participant 2, for example, stated:

> Sometimes aboriginal peoples tend to not want to brag as much about what they're doing and sometimes it's really tough to get someone to do a media interview or to get a student researcher to talk about what they're doing. I know that I've certainly experienced that difficulty [and] I chalk it up to a cultural difference.

The reticence of aboriginal scholars is naturalized as cultural. Again, this does not mean that all the participants were unaware of contested understandings of excellence.

> You know.... I think actually the truth is that it will be a preponderance of men and that's going to be no surprise to you as you probably are aware in the last round of CRCs[2] they were all men, right? (Participant 2)

Participant 3 explained that the preponderance of male media subjects was the lack of women experts in fields, but that this changing. She provided the example of a Black woman that they included in media coverage about research in Africa, even though a male colleague was "a much bigger deal." She also cited the example of putting a woman on stage when a large health research centre was opened, along with a male and female student. "That was deliberate because we wanted to show that women are in research" (Participant 3).

Participants did mention how much easier it is to represent STEM fields than social science or humanities; for example, how do you represent a scholar working on issues of poverty without being stereotypical and showing visuals of interest to "core" audiences? Participant 11 explained:

> Gender, cultural diversity for sure, you can't always depict this in an image; it depends on what type of image you're doing, but definitely diversity in discipline. Also, and this doesn't come across in an image either, but in the terms of the stories we tell, it's really important to feature stories about international students.

Again, international students are central to revenue, reputation management and rankings. Through my interviews, two things became evident. First, rankings, branding and reputation management are integrally related to the competition for students, government and industry funding. Second, the commitment of many public affairs workers to make public the importance of academic research to wider audiences is genuine and strong.

Senior public affairs workers are boundary setters. They play an important role in determining what and who is seen as a good researcher and good student. As we can see from this chapter, there are literal boundaries, and there are the more symbolic but not less important ones. The literal boundaries are the physical spaces between universities and cities or towns and the geographic borders universities want to cross by recruiting international students. But PA professionals are also setting, negotiating and battling over symbolic boundaries, too; indeed, they are involved in determining what the university should be. They negotiate and navigate boundaries about ideas that can be quite problematic and divisive In particular, many faculty attempt to thwart the efforts of PA workers to convey an impression of a unified university brand by insisting on speaking about their work without mention of the university brand, or by promoting their own individual scholarly brand.

Again, public affairs in universities often involve work that is discursively and practically located on two conflicting normative trajectories. On one hand, public affairs staff can help academics reach broader audiences and go beyond peer-reviewed journals to become important players in expanding conversations that impact people from local to global levels. This work is important, and public affairs workers often have skills academics may not have in communicating to diverse audiences. On the other hand, however, public affairs can be about narrowing academic and public conversations to core areas that align with knowledge relevant only if it results in economic accumulation. At a time when the world must confront crises of growing inequity and climate change, such an alignment defeats the purpose of universities as places of thinking and researching to find new ways of knowing and being. The question – to which I turn next – remains: How do we expand conversations about knowledge and public education in a democratic and pluralistic society by understanding existing practices in PA offices?

Conclusion

When giving a talk about rankings at a university in India, I began by saying that I'm from a top-ranked institution, and I admit that when I see UBC is still in the top 50, part of me is relieved. A high ranking means more opportunities for faculty and students – privilege tends to beget more privilege. At the same time, I ask myself: What do people really know about my university beyond rankings, or about the 97 to 99% of universities that are not ranked by the international rankings? At the talk in India, I asked, what do rankings leave out? A lively discussion ensued. What would it look like if equity was one of the indicators of excellence? One professor chuckled, "Well Harvard wouldn't be at the top." Someone else laughed and said, "Yes, we would be ranked highly – higher than Harvard." There was laughter, but their points deserve serious consideration. They asked questions about the responsibility of the university to their particular contexts and communities. Rankings institutionalize certain forms of knowledge in the name of globalization and internationalization.

Research pointing to the methodological, epistemological and ontological problems with rankings is extensive, yet the impact of university league tables continues to grow. Understanding this influence requires analysis of how rankings and mediatized text interact with the larger narratives around globalization and competition. Rankings are often presented as the consumer's right to know, but an illusion of neutrality obscures a "politics of information." Indeed, rankings seem to be creating a kind of "policy panic" in higher education: If Western universities do not serve the knowledge economy, America and Europe will soon be passed by China and India.

Mediatized rankings contribute to transforming knowledge into a commodity that can be measured, ranked and resourced – making much of the work of a university invisible. Ironically, mediatized rankings and university websites create a hyper-real sense of the university: Everything appears to be visible and transparent through tables, charts, happy-looking students, and serious-looking journalists and experts. University websites, however, are not merely an information venue but a form of politics. What information is highlighted? How many clicks does it take to get to information? What images are used to represent information? Who are the experts displayed on these websites that analyze information about excellence in education? What demographic do they represent? What fields of study? These are not merely technical but political decisions that rankers, universities and media make in relation to the brand of a university. What is relevant to the brand is important, but perhaps even more important are the forms of knowledge that are seen as immaterial or detrimental to the brand and how this exclusion limits the knowledge available to society. Özbilgin poses important questions:

> If we are engaged scholars, what are we engaged with, careerist ambitions or pursuit of knowledge? Can we reconcile these two ambitions? What prevents us from developing research quality measures that take account of the wider impact of our research rather than simply focusing on citations? (56: p. 120)

Understanding the use of rankings requires analysis of mediatization as a meta-process that is central to marketization of higher education. A number of critical policy and institutional analysts point to how the questions we ask change when the market is accepted as a common-sense foundation for education; research focuses on "Have we met our performance targets?" instead of "Who chose these indicators and why? And who is left out and why?" In addition, questions of who benefits from research do not play into the rankings: Do the rich get richer? Do the poor get poorer? Does the research play a transformative role in the lives of people or does it play a role in worsening their circumstances?

Workshops on branding the self abound. While at one time, faculty might wear a particular academic gown to show where they belonged within the university hierarchy, now faculty can wear what they wish – but in some ways there is a restoration of uniform through branded institutional media. Robert Giacalone argues academics are forgetting their responsibilities, instead conforming to logics antithetical to rigorous academic work.

> An unfortunate effect of our professional amnesia is a disconnection with the realities of our world and all that preceded us. Having

forgotten the assumptions that were the underpinning of our profession, we redirected our focus from producing quality work toward succeeding within a metrics-based reality, a metricality, where quality is narrowly and artificially defined. (203: p. 124)

Ranking is not simply technical. Rankings, as Page and Cramer (204) argue, raise moral questions: Research on stereotyping clearly shows that the stigmatization of people has a negative impact, so going to a low-ranking school may affect a student's economic prospects, but it also impacts their identity. Of course, the idea of schooling as a sign of distinction or commonness is not new: Bourdieu, for example, details the ways in which cultural and symbolic capital in education are manifest and intergenerational. Young people with cultural capital are more likely to envision themselves as students at an elite university than are students from a lower-income background, and high-income students are also more likely to have parents with the capital to help them successfully navigate the admissions process. Ironically, rankings can be seen as part of a backlash to increasing access to higher education and a marker of distinction. Rankings provide a way for those with cultural capital to say to those without: "You may have gone to a university, but you did not go to a highly ranked one." What is important to remember is that rankings provide choice for some – but not for the majority of the world's population. In fact, rankings can actually contribute to decreasing access to HEIs as industry and government put more money into the already rich institutions in hopes of getting them in the top 200.

Saleem Badat points out the connection between the modernist rationalizations of knowledge and contemporary university rankings:

If modernization theory depicts Western capitalist societies as the apex of modernity, global university rankings present the *world-class university* – essentially North American and European institutions – as the pinnacle and goal of all higher education development (205: p. 246).

In effect, new mediatized discourses draw on old narratives of educational excellence as a visible demonstration of distinction and superiority.

Branding and boundaries

Branding taps into powerful narratives of ranking everything from ice cream to doctoral education. Rankers are an important part of remixing discourse and structures that historically have been seen as separate:

Socrates, Walmart and academics – all appear part of capital accumulation. While the discourses of market are not hidden on the sites of rankers, particularly QS and THEWUR, what is largely absent are answers to questions such as: What are the financial costs of this spectacle to universities? How are these costs downloaded to students in the form of increased tuition fees? What are the financial costs to faculties, particularly those that are not revenue-generating?

University public affairs officers have recently become important players in the negotiation of the relationship between universities and ranking organizations. Communications workers become choreographers who determine which academics to put on stage, how to highlight the brand of a university and what to focus on, and how to permeate the boundaries that were previously more firm between academic research, industry and government. Ranking makes visibility a central concern for universities, changing relationships in consequence; for example, the role of media is heightened and alumni become revenue sources and reputation promoters.

What is most interesting about looking at university websites is the spin given to contradictory aims. Universities often speak about commitment to community, to the environment, and sometimes to indigenous people – and at the same time lay claim to being global institutions of higher education, economic engines and patent generators. What happens if a researcher creates something that is harmful to the environment? What if they create technology for weapon systems that will kill communities? How are these contradictory ideals of the university and what it means to be world class worked out?

Can we go beyond rankings?

Although universities contribute data and media for rankers and monopolistic publishers, there has been some effective resistance. Filip Vostal & Susan Robertson (206) suggest that the academy look to "non-capitalist social innovation and strategically deploy temporalities to secure a slowing down of resource depletion, or a pacing up of political awareness" (p. 31). Their work implies that despite pressure to conform, there is room for agency. Thousands of academics, for example, pushed Elsevier to withdraw support for a bill that would limit the ability of academics to freely share their work (207). Further, while HEI leadership in South Africa pays attention to rankings, it also challenges their inequity; Adam Habib explains, "A more active and nuanced version of this response bemoans the current state of affairs, but tries to fight back by trying to keep at bay the worse consequences of corporatization dynamics." An "alternative response," which Habib prefers, "is a proactive engagement with the context one finds oneself in with a view to subverting it in the long term" (185: p. 17). Here Habib acknowledges that the choices universities make around rankings are not mere common sense, but importantly political. The question is how to engage the political to influence debate and, ultimately, educational policy.

Media logics constrain spaces to conduct research and study diverse forms of frequently marginalized knowledge. While mediatization, similar to other meta-processes, is widespread, how it is experienced and implemented varies with context, and the process of convincing faculty and students to become a brand is not without tensions that can be exploited. For a university to present itself as purely market driven, for example, is a risky business and depends on faculty to see themselves as centrally knowledge economy workers – not likely. Academics have significant power to influence the directions of their universities if they choose to work together.

Finding different and more egalitarian ways of being with one other is urgent, and requires going beyond media and market logics and beyond Euro-American-centered knowledge and ways of determining the legitimacy of knowledge. Obviously Western knowledge is not homogenous, but there is something wrong with academia when we accept that scholarly excellence is predicated on writing in English. There is something wrong when academics from Asia and Africa talk about the immense pressure they are under to publish in English, in Western journals and about issues Westerners will be interested in so that they can raise the ranking of their respective institutions. There is something wrong when these scholars cannot access many relevant academic journals. There is something wrong when White male privilege largely determines what counts as legitimate and important knowledge. Opening ways of knowing goes beyond the university as a place to debate issues of material justice to understanding the university as a place to debate what Santos refers to as cognitive justice (208, 209).

An alternative to ranking systems requires the support of boundary workers. It also requires moving beyond seeing academics as liabilities and assets based on market risks and opportunities (210). Academics are often socialized to talk about their work exclusively to one other and boundary workers can help academics communicate to diverse audiences. The important question then becomes: How do we engage publics that are currently excluded or marginalized in discussions about what knowledge counts in defining good higher education?

Beginning and expanding conversations about education requires creating dialogic spaces not just for critique but for emotion. What are the very real fears and hopes that rankings provoke? The issue is enormously complicated. Indeed, it is understandable that university leaders, faculty and students pay so much attention to rankings: A student might not get a better education at an Ivy League school, but if an employer's perception is that they did, that student may end up with very different career opportunities. University leaders understand that despite the flaws of ranking, rankings influence decisions of policymakers and stakeholders; currently leaders ignore rankings at their peril – and to the detriment of the entire university community.

What can be done?

Merely criticizing branding and mediatization of higher education does not provide alternatives. Academics have a moral responsibility to communicate outside of academia and to understand the rights and needs of parents, students and society to know what goes on in universities and how they can participate. There are many examples of academics who successfully straddle the spaces between universities, communities and media, including bell hooks, Chinua Achebe, Noam Chomsky, Vibhuti Patel, Linda Tuhiwai Smith, Prem Chowdhry, Ngugi wa Thiong'o, and the late Maya Angelou and Edward Said. They did not seek to become media personalities, but to be public intellectuals exercising their responsibility to expand and deepen important conversations. Sometimes they work with public or corporate media; sometimes with independent media.

Does the greater reliance on mediatization and branding limit the ability of academics to challenge narratives about education as merely a private good? What makes the public intellectual significant, as I mention above, is that they are grounded in a particular location and the language of that place. They do not pretend to be an intellectual that could be in any place at any time with universal knowledge. Through their humility, they expand conversations in specific places and allow others opportunities to imagine themselves in other times and other places. Such scholarship is about understanding new knowledge, building on it and creating new insights. Asserting that there is only one way of knowing excellence – ranking – reduces scholarly excellence to a best brand.

We need to look to the many academics who have played a major role in collaborating with media and community groups to expand important conversations. Journalists can also play a role in framing public debate about what good education is and in challenging academics to look at the reproduction of inequities within universities. People like Shari Graydon have developed approaches to provide journalists with alternatives to the usual digital rolodex of sources: Graydon noticed that most expert sources cited by media were male and so she created Informed Opinions, which trains women academics to engage with media (http://www.informedopinions.org/).

Tenured professors have both the expertise and responsibility to challenge the underpinnings of rankings. We can look to academic-activists, such as Nobel Prize winner Randy Schekman, who have done this, or the groups of academics and activists who fought legislation that would prohibit American-funded researchers from freely sharing their results if they had been sponsored with federal funds.

Students and parents also might look for what is educationally important to them, but missing from ranking tables: Are they passionate about human rights or climate change? Do local communities matter? Is there evidence that universities practice what they preach? If the rankings aren't answering their questions, they might contact institutions of interest and ask them to post information on issues that are important to them.

Ultimately, we do have to acknowledge that university leaders and government policymakers are in a tough spot. Rankings are part of the global discourse on higher education, and this makes pragmatic resistance difficult. Political and university leaders live and die by understanding the zeitgeist of their moment, and to appear out of sync with what is seen as common sense can be career suicide. However, we can look to countries such as South Africa that do not ignore rankings, but communicate an expanded vision of what education is and could be. Educational policy is never inevitable, but based in political choices. Universities can claim that rankings provide an objective way to make tough resource allocation decisions in a tough economy, but no policy decision is objective; such decisions are always based in values relative to who and what is important. More work is needed to make transparent these decisions about winners and losers.

In sum, mediatized ranking and branding are restructuring higher education, but the continued march towards the corporate universities is not inevitable. To maintain a space for education that is distinct from the corporate world requires strategically connecting research and activism.

Connecting research and activism for education

Universities and academics need to use their knowledge to open up new spaces of exploration and action that focus on the nexus between mediatization, rankings and branding.

More research is needed to understand how media coverage impacts education and how universities attempt to influence reputation through adopting media formats and narratives. This book represents an exploration into mediatization and HE rankings. I studied universities located at the highest rank in their respective contexts; future studies are needed that examine how universities in the middle or bottom of the rankings are impacted. For example, what are the implications for their identity and how they survive? There is also need for global studies that look at the approximately 98% of universities that are not included in the Big Three ranking systems: How do these people acquiesce and resist? How do they create media to offer counter-narratives or attempt to move policymakers to expand their understanding of what counts as a good and worthwhile education?

Parents and students need information about post-secondary options and how to access different opportunities. Further research is needed about how to provide fulsome, respectful and relevant information to parents and students that assists them in decision-making. A number of academic blogs have gained traction and expanded conversations about rankings. Research in collaboration with journalists and journalism scholars is needed about alternatives to rankings that can contribute to better conversations about what education is and could be.

There are many cogent critiques of rankings, monopolistic journalism practices, impact factors and misuse of technology. What is needed, however, is to bring this work together to form an integrated study of rankings as an emerging economic sector that is reshaping education. The denseness of the network between rankers, databases, media and business requires greater study, particularly to find data to determine the profits gained from rankings – and their cost to education.

The whole area of rankings as an economic sector requires more research. Far more work is needed to assess the actual costs of rankings in higher education. How many dollars do universities spend to collect and organize data for a ranker, which is often sold back to the universities in the form of proprietary benchmarking and other tools? How much do universities spend on ranking management, including hiring staff and consultants, travelling to reputation management conferences, advertising, and completing reputation surveys? How many communication, marketing and branding dollars are focused on rankings? What evidence is there this money is improving university research and educational offerings?

Perhaps using a crowdsourcing model to collect, share and analyze information from different universities could provide a more accurate picture than we currently have concerning the real costs of rankings to education.

More research is needed that examines the intersecting fields of government, media, education and industry. How do players move between and across fields? How does this movement impact higher education policy from international to institutional levels? What has emerged from this book is that ranking is not an isolated activity, but enmeshed in government, media, education and industry, and in this way we see the emergence of rankings as a field of power.

Rankings are a new economic sector, but arguably the success of ranking is based in old narratives of imperialism. Breaking out of these narratives requires the theories of diverse communities that can also, as Gill et al. suggest, challenge the "theorists of the academy" (212: p. 2).

Finally, students have been at the forefront in challenging inequities in higher education and the marketization of higher education. Research that brings together academic research and activism is crucial to sustaining and expanding conversations about different ways of thinking about and creating spaces for education.

Appendix 1 Research Design, Methodology and Researcher's Perspective

This appendix describes how the different data were collected, analyzed, and presented. This is a qualitative study that drew on Luc Pauwel's (209) work in multimodal analysis of websites and critical discourse analysis (CDA). Data sources included semi-structured interviews, government and university documents related to branding and/or university rankings and the websites of 13 universities, three rankers and IREG, an organization charged with ascertaining the quality of rankings. The study grew out of an article I wrote for *Globalisation, Societies and Education* (214); my previous studies examined the role of media in educational policy, and encompassed interviews with elected officials, senior bureaucrats and journalists and document analysts. Prior to becoming an academic, I worked as a communications director for an office that investigated child fatalities and the quality of care for children in government; before this, I was an advisor to a minister of education in British Columbia. Through these experiences, I became interested in the powerful role of media in educational policy. I have examined the role of testing in media coverage of education and am interested in how academics and journalists with a commitment to equity can inform each other about ways to expand the public discussions about policy alternatives. My curiosity about rankings developed from frequently hearing about the importance of rankings from students and from academics.

Similar to Patricia Burch, who examined the hidden markets of K–12 education, I draw on a number of methodologies (213). Instead of focusing on K–12 policy as something that occurs in consultation between government, teachers and local authorities, she analyzed policy and trade documents and interviews to show how the trillion-dollar private education industry is now central to policymaking in the US.

Chapters 1 and 2

The literature on HE rankings is extensive. I focused my literature review on higher education policy and marketing, comparative higher education, and critical higher education educational policy literature. I did look at some of the bibliometric literature to better understand the role of reporting on bibliometric data through mediatized rankings, but this was not my focus. There is a small, but growing, literature on mediatization and education, which I drew upon; however, I also looked to the more expansive literature on mediatization in political communication and media studies. All publications included in my literature review are in English. In addition to peer-reviewed studies and relevant blogs (e.g., globalhighered.wordpress.com), HE general audience publications such as the *Chronicle of Higher Education* and *Inside Higher Education* were analyzed.

Analysis of websites (Chapters 3, 4, 5)

Visualization has taken on new importance with the growth of websites as primary marketing tools for universities and rankers. The advantage of critical discourse analysis as an analytic tool is the focus on understanding text, including graphic text in its socio-political context. Luc Pauwels (209) suggests that critical discourse analysis is useful for multimedia research; notwithstanding, for him, websites require new modes of analysis that account for the multimedia and multi-authored nature of websites as well as algorithms used for search functions that might bring some information to the forefront and bury other information. In particular he suggests six possible phases for multimodal analysis of websites (p. 252):

(1) "Preservation of first impressions and reactions"

Sometimes my first impression of a site was that it was dynamic and exciting; however, after hours of analyzing a site I forgot this. These first impressions are important to thinking through the navigation of a site and use of images and sound to draw a viewer in; for example, how my eye was drawn to certain navigation features changed from the first hour of viewing a site to the 10th or 11th hour; This is important to understanding how prospective students might view a website in contrast to a faculty member looking for online library resources.

(2) "Inventory of salient features and topics"

Here I looked at what images and text were clustered together and compared this across sites. For example, university websites that I examined in Canada, the US and UK included a number of still images and rotating videos and images in comparison to universities in India and China. Also examined is "negative analysis" (p. 256), that is, people, things and topics not represented. Here again, I noted an absence of people with visible disabilities and, over the websites, more of a focus on Science, Technology, Engineering and Mathematics (STEM) areas. This was useful for looking at navigation bars. How many clicks did it take to get to different topics? What was the font for different information categories? I also drew on Kress and van Leeuwen (137) to look at the typography, the saturation of color, hue, and mixing of color to understand how the importance of information was visually denoted.

(3) "In-depth analysis of content and formal choices"

I looked at verbal and written signifiers separately and in relation to audio and images. A website contains numerous webpages that may focus on multiple audiences (e.g., webpages focused on student services versus pages aimed at potential funders). Communicating to multiple audiences also requires the use of different forms of address (e.g., communicating to prospective students versus prospective industry partners). Typographic signifiers also provided cues as to the hierarchy of information. Larger text located in the center of the page is obviously easier to locate than small text at the bottom of a page. Visual signifiers, such as an image of a lion to show strength and superiority, were analyzed in relation to text about excellence. Audio or "sonic signifiers" are also important for imparting narrative authority or a celebration of fun for prospective students looking at different options (e.g., the Hollywood countdown evident in the 2011–2012 THEWUR versus the serious interview in 2014–2015 provides different sonic signifiers to the audience). Looking at what is absent (e.g., no images of people with visible disabilities) assists in examining the framing of dominant narratives and who and what it might be seen as taboo to make visual.

(4) "embedded point(s) of view or 'voice' and implied audience(s) purposes"

I examined cues for whether a particular video or article was written for prospective students and parents or for prospective industry funders, government or faculty members. What were the differences across websites within and across cultural contexts? How did universities demonstrate being situated in a particular local space and also a mobile, global world? Use of language and graphics of clubs and support, for example, often indicated content aimed at students, whereas tables and charts frequently denoted information for industry or government. Images of famous alumni often involved people who had gained great financial wealth. A central part of this phase of analysis was to understand the point of view (POV): A website may have many points of view but embedded are dominant points of view.

Acquiring and sustaining different audiences may involve different key messages – and sometimes what can appear to be contradictory messages. A message aimed at students might focus on the fun lifestyle a campus offers and one for industry on the hard-working, driven students and faculty; however, despite multiple audiences, the websites were clearly created with a hierarchy of expected visitors or users.

(5) "analysis of information, organization and Spatial Priming Strategies"

Here I looked at the navigational choices that provide windows to what information is most to least important. How are the producers of a website hoping audiences will move through it? What do they want audiences to see first? I analyzed what was on the primary navigation bar: Who and what are given the most space? Where was space given? Who appears where (e.g., males in relation to females)? Websites include a gamut of priming tools and strategies (most viewed videos, news, eye catchers, banners, pop-ups, internal links) (p. 258). Tools can provide clues to the beliefs and values that underlie a website through looking at what strategies are used. I also examined external links to other organizations that often provided an understanding of networks of power, social media links and other interactive features.

(6) "contextual analysis, provenance and inference"

Unlike identifying the author of a book, determining who created a particular website is challenging; for example, a web designer might use a platform such as SquareSpace to create a site, but SquareSpace sets the parameters for what the designer can and can't do. Some websites might require a subscription or have different levels of access. A website design includes many cultural, technological and political hierarchies.

Rankings are interpreted through local contexts but also through the flow of capital and people. I drew on Machin (14) to analyze whether the textual and visual signifiers surrounding rankings point to the growth of a global visual language.

Chapter 3

The Academic Ranking of World Universities (ARWU), the Times Higher Education World University Ranking (THEWUR) and Quacquarelli Symonds (QS) are sometimes referred to as the "Big Three." These rankings are widely reported and used by audiences as varied as students making choices about which university to attend to national policymakers. I analyzed the websites using the steps described above. I began by taking snapshots of the homepages of each ranker. I then downloaded documents and reports produced by QS, THEWUR or ARWU on their methodology, as well as any press releases, news reports, financial reports, and biographical information about senior staff and advisory members. All the information gathered about board members is in the public domain; I used this information to search for additional data to analyze the movement of people between and across rankings and other networks of power (e.g., government). I used a code sheet to analyze placement of information on the website: In particular, what was on the homepage "above" and "below" the fold, the navigation bars, and how many clicks did it take to get to information? Based on my analysis, I added IREG to get a better understanding of movement across ranking organizations and between ranking organizations and a ranking regulator.

Second, I drew on Bourdieu's concepts of field, habitus and capital to uncover networks of power and movement between and across fields. I examined this based on advisory board membership and senior staff. With the biographies, I searched for other information about advisory members, including publications they have written and their work history. I looked at publically available financial statements and media reports about the rankings and financial status of rankers (e.g., *Forbes*).

I also analyzed other products owned by rankers – particularly related to the education sector, such as citation databases and academic journals. The analysis of other holdings or partnerships led to an analysis of Elsevier's Scopus and Thomson Reuters' Web of Science (WOS). Analysis of these websites, in turn, led to a review of academic and news pieces and government policy documents on the role of Elsevier and the WOS in higher education. I focused on documents that were publicly available because my interest is in looking at the public stories rankers tell about themselves.

Chapter 4

This chapter examines the semiotics of education using World University Rankings (THEWUR) as a case study. The first part of the chapter is based on a paper that I wrote and published in *Globalisation, Societies and Education* (214), which focused on the 2011–2012 THEWUR ranking. This chapter compares the 2011–2012 THEWUR website to the 2014–2015 THEWUR website. I followed the process provided by Pauwels (see above section on 'Analysis of websites').

Chapter 5

The process for analysis of university websites was as follows: First, I chose websites of the first-ranked institutions in a country, based on the three ranking systems. Obviously these universities are not representative of universities in their respective national context. My aim was to understand how top-ranked institutions in six very different contexts represent their institution in relation to their ranking and the similarities and differences in how they do this within a national context and across the six national contexts of the 13 universities included in this chapter. Unlike the other five countries, in Canada, the University of Toronto was ranked #1 by each of the Big Three. For the sake of comparison, I chose to also include the University of British Columbia, which often ranks 2nd in Canada in these rankings. This resulted in a selection of 13 universities.

Second, my research assistants, Leticia Pamela Garcia and Yu Guo, took a snapshot of the university homepage and section for prospective students in December 2014 and December 2007. Kem Saichaie, in his comprehensive dissertation on American university websites, argues the homepage of a university website is "where institutions repeatedly foreground the relevance of the institution by showcasing how it is distinctive" (157: p. 76).

Third, we searched for mentions of rankings anywhere on the university websites and took snapshots of pages with reference to rankings. In December, universities often do pieces on what they see as the most significant news for their institution at the closing of the calendar year. Using Wayback Internet Archive, we searched archives of the same university homepages from 2007. (In 2007, there were vocal protests to rankings in much of the world, and many universities refused to participate.) I decided to use only 2014 in this chapter. For 2007 images did not always show up with Wayback, and for some universities I was able to access more information than for others. I decided this posed issues for making statements about differences in the pages; however, I did note there is a need for more study to systematically analyze changes in website politics and consistent archiving of website data to make this possible.

Fourth, my research assistant Yu Guo and I looked at each website and wrote down our first impressions. We did this independently. We looked at our first impression about who and what was seen as important knowledge and what if any connections to rankings were evident. We then went to the homepage dedicated to the recruitment of prospective students and followed the same process.

Fifth, we used the search function for each university website to look for one of the following terms or combinations of terms: ranking and Times Higher Education, rankings and ARWU, rankings and Shanghai Ranking, rankings and QS, University rankings, league table, world ranking, world-class.

Sixth, we developed and redefined codes, drawing on Pauwels and Kress and van Leeuwen. We paid attention to markers of class, race, gender, disability and field of study.

Seventh, for the Chinese University website my research assistant Yu Guo, who is fluent in Mandarin and English, translated the Chinese version of the pages to English for me. I did my own further analysis, following the steps outlined by Pauwels.

I chose to focus on China, South Africa, India, the US, the UK and Canada for the following reasons. China, India and South Africa are part of the new BRICS and Emerging Economies ranking. I wanted to analyze dynamics across these contexts as the number of rankings targeting BRICS countries increase. In addition, China and India are major suppliers of international students to Canada, the US and UK; India and China are also host countries for a growing number of international students, particularly from Africa and other parts of Asia. South Africa is the only country that has universities in each of the Big Three rankings. Furthermore, the rules governing HE and funding have been transformed since the relatively recent end of apartheid. South Africa is a host country of many international students throughout Africa.

The ARWU, the first popular international rankings system, was created at a Chinese university. The Times Higher Education ranking comes out of the UK, as does the QS. The UK has been a leader in using rankings for policy decision-making and competes with the US for top status. Decision-making is highly influenced by rankings in the US, which is the home of a number of ranking systems. Canada has had a recent shift in government policy to increase the number of international students and involvement of Canadian universities in education as a major export.

My research team searched for government websites and documents that related to education and ranking in Canada, India, South Africa, the US and the UK. This included documents found in ministries of education but also in areas of international trade. Yu Guo looked up particular references to the rankings in the Chinese Ministry of Education. I also analyzed publicly available minutes from governing bodies of universities (e.g., university senates), and government sources and media sources around issues of ranking and branding.

Chapter 6

Fisher and Atkinson-Grosjean (2002) describe the role of industry-liaison offices as doing "boundary work" in their role of commercializing academic research. Public affairs (PA) offices play a similar and interconnected role in translating academic research and mobilizing knowledge across institutional and public settings. Little study has been given to the processes of how these decisions are actually made.

This chapter took a phenomenological approach. I was interested in how these boundary workers understood their role within the university context and the meanings they made out of this role. I deliberately decided to focus on Canada for a few reasons: First, I'm from Canada, and it is the context I am most familiar with; second, mediatization is a global meta-process, but how it is experienced and understood is local; third, there is a dearth of research that focuses on the nexus between Canadian higher education and media.

I conducted semi-structured interviews with senior public affairs staff at research universities in Canada. All PA staff at the most senior level in the U15 (largest Canadian research universities) were invited to participate. In some universities, the title of director is used, and in others manager or VP. I use the terms PA workers, staff and participants throughout the chapter, rather than breaking up a small group by specific title. I did so to maintain anonymity of participants. Contact information was acquired through university directories. After obtaining approval from UBC's Behavioral Research and Ethics Board, PA directors were sent a personal email inviting them to participate. I interviewed each participant once for 60 to 90 minutes; most interviews were by phone or Skype. Interviews took place between 2012 and 2014. The interviews focused on the following questions:

1. How do PA directors describe characteristics of newsworthy academics and research?
2. How do PA directors in Tier 1 Canadian institutions conceptualize the role of public affairs departments among members of the academic community within the university and in relation to publics and institutions situated outside of the university?
3. How do PA directors think through questions of inclusion and exclusion regarding who should and should not be represented on university websites in relation to their work?

The issue of rankings came up with many interviewees in relation to talking to publics outside the university and student recruitment. I selected research-intensive schools for comparability of institutional drivers and networks of power and interviewed eleven PA senior staff from nine institutions. However, two (from the same institution) left the institution and I was unable to locate them; they had provided only work emails which, when I attempted to send the transcript, bounced back to me. The sound quality of the third interview was substandard (the interview took place over Skype). The extensive notes I took from these interviews informed this research. Notwithstanding, there are no quotes from these participants included in my narrative.

Appendix 2 Biographies for Rankers and IREG Advisory Board Members

ARWU Advisory	http://www.shanghairanking.com/aboutiab.html
IREG	http://www.ireg-observatory.org/index.php?option=com_content&task=blogcategory&id=23&Itemid=239
QS Advisory Committee	http://www.iu.qs.com/qs-advisory-board/
TES Global	http://www.tesglobal.com/advisory-board

Notes

2 Seeing Is Believing: University Websites

1. Great Britain pound sterling.
2. Chapter 6 will elaborate on the work of boundary workers in public relations at Canadian universities.
3. The quality of seeming to be true according to one's intuition, opinion, or perception without regard to logic, factual evidence, or the like: The growing trend of truthiness as opposed to truth. Dictionary.com
4. Used to measure how many people come to a website, how long they stay on different pages, and some demographic details such as the country the site is being viewed from.

3 Who Is Watching the Watchdogs? The Business of Rankings

1. Science, Technology, Engineering and Mathematics.

4 Visualizing Excellence: The Times Higher Education Ranking

1. The part of this chapter dealing with the 2011–2012 ranking was previously published in *Globalisation, Societies and Education* (214). In this paper I referred to the THE Ranking. In this chapter, to improve readability I refer to the same ranking using THEWUR. THEWUR is part of the Times Higher Education website.
2. See Appendix 1 for details on methodology used for this chapter.
3. IDP was founded in 1969. At first it was called the Australia Asian Universities' Cooperation Scheme, and in the 1980s the organization became the International Development Program, www.idp.com.

5 Mediatization and University Websites

1. Google Analytics tracks website traffic and data. It can also provide "cohort analysis"; i.e., demographic information about a viewer.
2. The Russell Group consists of 24 UK research institutions. Russell refers to Russell Square – famous for its presence in a number of novels, including Thackeray's *Vanity Fair*. The Russell Group denotes elite, research-focused institutions. Two-thirds of research grants and contracts go to the Russell Group, and over 56% of doctoral degrees are granted by them. The group also produced a video about what a difference world-class universities make and

the superiority of the UK in producing world-class universities and researchers (17).

6   Boundary Workers: University Public Affairs Workers

1. Bay Street refers to a major business center in Toronto, Canada.
2. Canadian Research Chairs – prestigious positions largely funded by the Canadian government.

Bibliography

1. TPG [Internet]. [cited April 10, 2015]. Available from: https://tpg.com/.
2. Krotz F. The meta-process of 'mediatization' as a conceptual frame. *Glob Media Commun.* 2007; 3(3):256–260.
3. Chan-Olmsted SM, Chang B-H. Diversification Strategy of Global Media Conglomerates: Examining Its Patterns and Determinants. *J Media Econ.* 2003; 16(4):213–233.
4. Altbach PG, Knight J. The internationalization of higher education: Motivations and realities. *J Stud Int Educ.* 2007; 11(3–4):290–305.
5. Altbach PG. Rankings season is here. The international imperative in higher education [Internet]. Springer; 2013 [cited November 21, 2014]. p. 81–88. Available from: http://link.springer.com/chapter/10.1007/978–94–6209–338–6_19.
6. Crawford SP. *Captive Audience: The Telecom Industry and Monopoly Power in the New Gilded Age.* Yale University Press; 2013. 370 p.
7. Rauhvargers A. Global university rankings and their impact: report II. Brussels: European University Association; 2013.
8. Online Etymology Dictionary [Internet]. [cited February 11, 2015]. Available from: http://www.etymonline.com/index.php?allowed_in_frame=0&search=brand&searchmode=none.
9. Hepp A. Mediatization and the "moulding force" of the media. 2012 [cited March` 23, 2014]; Available from: http://www.degruyter.com/dg/viewarticle/j$002fcommun.2012.37.1.issue-1$002fcommun-2012–0001$002fcommun-2012–0001.xml.
10. Altheide DL, Snow RP. *Media Logic.* Beverly Hills, California: SAGE Publications, Inc; 1979. 252 p.
11. Hazelkorn E. *Rankings and the Reshaping of Higher Education: The Battle for World-Class Excellence.* New York: Palgrave Macmillan; 2011. ix, 259 p.
12. Hazelkorn E. Reflections on a decade of global rankings: what we've learned and outstanding issues. *Eur J Educ.* 2014; 49(1):12–28.
13. Machin D. Building the world's visual language: The increasing global importance of image banks in corporate media. *Vis Commun.* 2004; 3(3):316–336.
14. Kirkness VJ, Barnhardt R. First nations and higher education: The four R's – respect, relevance, reciprocity, responsibility. *J Am Indian Educ.* 1991; 30(3):1–15.
15. *Getting In...Kindergarten* pt.1 [Internet]. 2008 [cited April 5, 2015]. Available from:https://www.youtube.com/watch?v=WsuIbYLpuZI&feature=youtube_gdata_player.
16. Debord G. *The Society of the Spectacle.* New York: Zone Books; 1994. 154 p.
17. Van Parijs P. European higher education under the spell of university rankings. *Ethical Perspect.* 2009; 16(2):189–206.
18. Longden B. *Ranking Indicators and Weights. University Rankings.* Dordrecht: Springer Netherlands; 2011. pp. 73–104.

19. Jump P. King Abdulaziz gets a rankings rise on the back of secondary measures. *Times Higher Education.* 2014; (2161):8.
20. Sauder M, Lancaster R. Do rankings matter? The effects of U.S. News & World Report Rankings on the admissions process of law schools. *Law Soc Rev.* 2006; 40(1):105–134.
21. Paradeise C, Thoenig J-C. Academic institutions in search of quality: Local orders and global standards. *Organ Stud.* 2013; 34(2):189–218.
22. Ridell S. Top university – downhill for humanities? Policing the future of higher education in the Finnish mainstream media. *Eur Educ Res J.* 2008; 7(3):289–307.
23. Redden E. Methodology of QS rankings comes under scrutiny. *Inside Higher Education* [Internet]. 2103 [cited March 12, 2015]. Available from: https://www.insidehighered.com/news/2013/05/29/methodology-qs-rankings-comes-under-scrutiny.
24. Bruni F. Promiscuous college come-ons. *The New York Times* [Internet]. November 22, 2014 [cited November 26, 2014]; Available from: http://www.nytimes.com/2014/11/23/opinion/sunday/frank-bruni-promiscuous-college-come-ons.html.
25. Bastedo MN, Bowman NA. U.S. News & World Report College Rankings: Modeling institutional effects on organizational reputation. *Am J Educ.* 2010; 116(2):163–183.
26. Lederman D. "Manipulating," Er, Influencing "U.S. News."*Inside Higher Education.* [Internet]. [cited March 27, 2015]. Available from: https://www.insidehighered.com/news/2009/06/03/rankings.
27. Chang GC, Osborn JR. Spectacular colleges and spectacular rankings: The "US News" rankings of American "best" colleges. *J Consum Cult.* 2005; 5(3):338–364.
28. Kornberger M Carter C. Manufacturing competition: how accounting practices shape strategy making in cities. *Account Audit Account J.* 2010; 23(3):325–349.
29. Samarasekera I. Rising up against rankings *Inside Higher Education.*[Internet]. 2007 [cited October 23, 2014]. Available from: https://www.insidehighered.com/views/2007/04/02/samarasekera.
30. Goral T. Rankings exodus may be tipping point. *University Business.* 2007; 10(8):12.
31. Bennett D. The way forward on college rankings. Remarks delivered to the Annapolis Group. Jun 20, 2007.
32. Salmi J, Saroyan A. League tables as policy instruments: Uses and misuses. *High Educ Manag Policy.* 2007; 19(2):31–68.
33. Cohen D. Asiaweek cancels controversial university survey [Internet]. *The Guardian.* [cited March 28, 2015]. Available from: http://www.theguardian.com/education/2001/aug/01/highereducation.uk.
34. Dill DD, Soo M. Academic quality, league tables, and public policy: A cross-national analysis of university ranking systems. *High Educ.* 2005; 49(4):495–533.
35. Wellen A. The $8.78 million maneuver. *The New York Times* [Internet]. 2005 Jul 31 [cited October 8, 2014]; Available from: http://www.nytimes.com/2005/07/31/education/edlife/wellen31.html.

36. Brighenti A. Visibility: A category for the social sciences. *Curr Sociol.* 2007; 55(3):323–342.
37. Boyd D, Crawford K. Critical questions for big data. *Inf Commun Soc.* 2012;15(5):662–679.
38. Beigel F. Introduction: Current tensions and trends in the World Scientific System. *Curr Sociol.* 2014; 62(5):617–625.
39. Latzer M, Hollnbuchner K, Just N, Saurwein F. The economics of algorithmic selection on the Internet. [Internet]. University of Zurich, Zurich; 2014. Available from: http://www.mediachange.ch/media/pdf/publications/economics_of_algorithmic_selection.pdf.
40. Kammer A. The mediatization of journalism. *MedieKultur J Media Commun Res.* 2014; 29(54):18 p.
41. Forgas JP, Laham SM. Halo effect. *Encyclopedia of Social Psychology* [Internet]. SAGE Publications, Inc.; 2007 [cited April 10, 2015]. Available from: http://knowledge.sagepub.com/view/socialpsychology/n248.xml.
42. Marginson S. Global university rankings: implications in general and for Australia. *J High Educ Policy Manag.* 2007; 29(2):131–42.
43. Hazelkorn E. How rankings are reshaping higher education. 2013 [cited Dec 31, 2013]; Available from: http://arrow.dit.ie/cgi/viewcontent.cgi?article=1023&context=cserbk.
44. Bolan LC, Robinson DJ. "Part of the university lexicon": Marketing and Ontario universities, 1990–2013. *Can J Commun.* 2013; 38(4):563–584.
45. Robertson S, Olds K. "Passing judgment": the role of credit rating agencies in the global governance of UK universities [Internet]. *Glob High Educ.* [cited March 3, 2015]. Available from: https://globalhighered.wordpress.com/2008/08/06/passing-judgement/.
46. Brodsky S. Feature: A brand-led reinvention of higher education [Internet]. Marketing Magazine. [cited 2015 Aug 5]. Available from: https://www.marketingmag.com.au/hubs-c/feature-a-brand-led-reinvention-of-higher-education/
47. Slaughter S, Cantwell B. Transatlantic moves to the market: The United States and the European Union. *High Educ.* 2012; 63(5):583–606.
48. Hassanein S, Yake M. Special comment: Increased policy focus on international students credit positive for Canadian universities. Moody's Investors Service; 2014 Aug. Report No.: 174041.
49. King R. Policy internationalization, national variety and governance: global models and network power in higher education states. *High Educ.* 2010; 60 (6): 583–594.
50. Howsoniko, KC. Drop in foreign student numbers: are UK universities too complacent? [Internet]. *The Guardian.* [cited April 4, 2015]. Available from: http://www.theguardian.com/higher-education-network/blog/2014/apr/04/drop-oreign-student-numbers-uk-universities-too-complacent.
51. Lo WYW. University rankings as a zoning technology: a Taiwanese perspective on an imaginary Greater China higher education region. *Glob Soc Educ.* 2013; 11(4):459–478.
52. Lo WYW. Theorising university rankings. *University Rankings* [Internet]. Springer Singapore; 2014 [cited October 27, 2014]. pp. 41–79. Available from: http://link.springer.com.ezproxy.library.ubc.ca/chapter/10.1007/978-981-4560-35-1_3.

53. Kang M. "State-guided" university reform and colonial conditions of knowledge production. *Inter-Asia Cult Stud.* 2009; 10(2):191–205.
54. Huang M-H. Opening the black box of QS World University Rankings. *Res Eval.* 2012; 21(1):71–78.
55. Ishikawa M. University rankings, global models, and emerging hegemony critical analysis from Japan. *J Stud Int Educ.* 2009; 13(2):159–173.
56. Özbilgin MF. From journal rankings to making sense of the world. *Acad Manag Learn Educ.* 2009; 8(1):113–121.
57. Altbach PG. Peripheries and centers: research universities in developing countries. *Asia Pac Educ Rev.* 2009; 10(1):15–27.
58. Aronczyk M, Powers D. *Blowing Up the Brand: Critical Perspectives on Promotional Culture.* Peter Lang; 2010, 352
59. Chapleo C, Carrillo Durán MV, Castillo Díaz A. Do UK universities communicate their brands effectively through their websites? *J Mark High Educ.* 2011; 21(1):25–46.
60. Ng CJW, Koller V. Deliberate conventional metaphor in images: The case of corporate branding discourse. *Metaphor Symb.* 2013; 28(3):131–147.
61. Bélanger CH, Syed S, Mount J. The make up of institutional branding: Who, what, how? *Tert Educ Manag.* 2007; 13(3):169–185.
62. Canadian universities launch startup incubator with Bombay Stock Exchange [Internet]. *Financial Post.* [cited April 6, 2015]. Available from: http://business. financialpost.com/entrepreneur/fp-startups/canadian-universities-launch-startup-incubator-with-bombay-stock-exchange.
63. Ruch RS, Keller G. *Higher Ed, Inc.: The Rise of the For-Profit University.* Baltimore: Johns Hopkins University Press; 2003. 200 p.
64. Lamb CW. *Marketing.* Cengage Learning; 2012. 714 p.
65. Hey big spender: how does your university's marketing budget compare? [Internet]. *The Australian.* [cited April 4, 2015]. Available from: http://www. theaustralian.com.au/higher-education/hey-big-spender-how-does-your-universitys-marketing-budget-compare/story-e6frgcjx-1226513104164.
66. Boffey D. From freshers to focus groups: how universities are learning to advertise [Internet]. *The Guardian.* [cited April 4, 2015]. Available from: http:// www.theguardian.com/education/2014/may/18/universities-turn-to-ad-man.
67. Rohan T. Groups want bad image of Penn State to go away. *The New York Times* [Internet]. 2013 September 16 [cited April 5, 2015]; Available from: http://www.nytimes.com/2013/09/17/sports/ncaafootball/groups-want-poor-image-of-penn-state-to-go-away.html.
68. Penn State loses first sponsor [Internet]. *The Chronicle Herald.* 2014 [cited April 5, 2015]. Available from: http://thechronicleherald.ca/sports/120635-penn-state-loses-first-sponsor.
69. Moody's downgrades Pennsylvania State University's long-term rating to Aa2 from Aa1, affecting $893 million of outstanding rated debt [Internet]. Moodys.com. [cited April 5, 2015]. Available from: https://www.moodys. com/research/Moodys-downgrades-Pennsylvania-State-Universitys-long-term-rating-to-Aa2 – PR_258616.
70. Copping David. A university's brand is of real commercial value. *Times Higher Education* [Internet]. THE World Reputation Ranking. n.d. [cited February 11, 2015]. Available from: http://www.timeshighereducation.co.uk. ezproxy.library.ubc.ca/world-university-rankings/2013/reputation-ranking/analysis/a-universitys-brand.

71. Gieryn TF. Boundary-Work and the demarcation of science from non-science: Strains and interests in professional ideologies of scientists. *Am Sociol Rev.* 1983; 48(6):781–795.
72. Fisher D, Atkinson-Grosjean J. Brokers on the boundary: Academy-industry liaison in Canadian universities. *High Educ.* 2002; 44(3/4):449–467.
73. Wedel JR. *Shadow Elite: How the World's New Power Brokers Undermine Democracy, Government, and the Free Market.* New York: Basic Books; 2011. 304 p.
74. Neumark V. What's in a name? The value of a good university brand [Internet]. *The Guardian.* [cited April 5, 2015]. Available from: http://www.theguardian. com/higher-education-network/blog/2012/apr/03/branding-universities.
75. Scheckman R. How journals like Nature, Cell and Science are damaging science. [Internet]. *The Guardian.* [cited April 4, 2015]. Available from: http:// www.theguardian.com/commentisfree/2013/dec/09/how-journals-nature-science-cell-damage-science.
76. World 100 Reputation Network | Managing the reputations of the World's leading universities [Internet]. [cited April 18, 2015]. Available from: http:// theworld100.com/.
77. Karisson A. Conference: How can Asian universities build a strong global brand? [Internet]. Elsevier Connect. 2014 [cited February 3, 2015]. Available from:http://www.elsevier.com/connect/conference-how-can-asian-universities-build-a-strong-global-reputation.
78. Kress GR. *Reading Images: The Grammar of Visual Design.* 2nd ed. Milton Park, Abingdon, Oxon; New York: Routledge; 2006. 291.
79. Rosen DE, Purinton E. Website design: Viewing the web as a cognitive landscape. *J Bus Res.* 2004; 57(7): 787–794.
80. Klassen ML. Lots of fun, not much work, and no hassles: Marketing images of higher education. *J Mark High Educ.* 2001; 10(2):11–26.
81. Wernick A. Rebranding Harvard. *Theory Cult Soc.* 2006; 23(2–3):566–567.
82. Callahan E. Cultural similarities and differences in the design of university web sites. *J Comput-Mediat Commun.*
83. Ng CJW. "We offer unparalleled flexibility": Purveying conceptual values in higher educational corporate branding. *Discourse Commun.* 2014; 8(4):391–410.
84. Ramasubramanian S, Gyure JF, Mursi NM. Impact of Internet images: Impression-formation effects of university web site images. *J Mark High Educ.* 2003; 12(2):49–68.
85. Xiong T. Discourse and marketization of higher education in China: The genre of advertisements for academic posts. *Discourse Soc.* 2012; 23(3):318–337.
86. Baudrillard J.. *The Gulf War Did Not Take Place* Indiana University Press; 1995. 100 p.
87. Pippert TD., Essenburg LJ., Matchett EJ. We've got minorities, yes we do: visual representations of racial and ethnic diversity in college recruitment materials. *J Mark High Educ.* 2013; 23(2):258–282.
88. Jillapalli RK., Jillapalli R. Do professors have customer-based brand equity? *J Mark High Educ.* 2014; 24(1):22–40.
89. Hazelkorn E. The obsession with rankings in tertiary education: Implications for public policy. *Higher Education Policy Research Unit*, Presentation Slides, World, Washington, DC, January 2015
90. Deacon D, Stanyer J. Mediatization: key concept or conceptual bandwagon? *Media Cult Soc.* 2014; 36(7):1032–1044.

91. Couldry N. Communicative figurations.| Working Paper| No. 3. 2013 [cited May 9, 2014]; Available from: http://www.kommunikative-figurationen.de/fileadmin/redak_kofi/Arbeitspapiere/CoFI_EWP_No-3_Couldry.pdf.

92. Rawolle S, Lingard B. The mediatization of the knowledge based economy: An Australian field based account. *Communications.* 2010; 35(3):269–286.

93. Colley H, Chadderton C, Nixon L. Collaboration and contestation in further and higher education partnerships in England: a Bourdieusian field analysis. *Crit Stud Educ.* 2014; 55(2):104–121.

94. ARWU. ARWU Methodology [Internet]. Available from: http://www.shanghairanking.com/ARWU-Methodology-2014.html.

95. Hazelkorn E. Rankings and the global reputation race. *New Dir High Educ.* 2014; (168):13–26.

96. Hvistendahl M. The man behind the world's most-watched college rankings. *Chronicle of Higher Education.* 2008; 55(8):A29–A29.

97. Bhattacharjee Y. Saudi universities offer cash in exchange for academic prestige. *Science.* 2011; 334(6061):1344–1345.

98. Docampo D. Reproducibility of the Shanghai academic ranking of world universities results. *Scientometrics.* 2013; 94(2):567–587.

99. Van Raan AFJ. Fatal attraction: Conceptual and methodological problems in the ranking of universities by bibliometric methods. *Scientometrics.* 2005; 62(1):133–143.

100. Florian RV. Irreproducibility of the results of the Shanghai academic ranking of world universities. *Scientometrics.* 2007; 72(1):25–32.

101. ARWU. About academic rankings of world universities [Internet]. Available from: http://www.shanghairanking.com/aboutarwu.html.

102. Lambert R, Great Britain, Treasury. Lambert review of business-university collaboration: final report. London: HM Treasury; 2003.

103. About QS [Internet]. *Top Universities.* [cited April 11, 2015]. Available from: http://www.topuniversities.com/about-qs.

104. Holmes R. The THES university rankings: are they really world class? *Asian J Univ Educ.* 2006; 2(1):1–14.

105. Understanding the methodology: QS World University Rankings [Internet]. *Top Universities.* [cited April 11, 2015]. Available from: http://www.topuniversities.com/university-rankings-articles/world-university-rankings/understanding-methodology-qs-world-university-rankings.

106. Hare J. Rankings agency QS targets league table guru Simon Marginson [Internet]. *The Australian.* [cited April 26, 2015]. Available from: http://www.theaustralian.com.au/higher-education/rankings-agency-qs-targets-league-table-guru-simon-marginson/story-e6frgcjx-1226662058026.

107. Ranking of unis is "bad science," says Simon Marginson [Internet]. *The Australian.* [cited April 26, 2015]. Available from: http://www.theaustralian.com.au/higher-education/ranking-of-unis-is-bad-science-says-simon-marginson/story-e6frgcjx-1226740536595.

108. Downing K. International rankings: A poisoned choice [Internet]. *University World News.* Available from: http://www.universityworldnews.com/article.php?story=20120320104648996.

109. Forsberg OJ, Payton ME. Analysis of battleground state presidential polling performances, 2004–2012. *Stat Public Policy.* 2015; 2 (1).

110. QS. QS intelligence unit guide to service pack [Internet]. 2013. Available from:http://www.iu.qs.com/wp-content/uploads/2013/10/7586-QSIU-Guide-to-Services-Pack-Oct-2013.pdf.

111. Guttenplan DD. Ratings at a Price for Smaller Universities. *The New York Times* [Internet]. 2012 December 30 [cited 2015 June 27]; Available from: http://www.nytimes.com/2012/12/31/world/europe/31iht-educlede31.html

112. QS-APPLE. The prime conference and exhibition for top international educators in Asia, Europe, America and Australasia [Internet]. [cited April 11, 2015]. Available from: http://www.qsapple.org/7thqsapple/about.php.

113. QS University Rankings: BRICS Methodology. [Internet]. *Top Universities*. [cited April 8, 2015]. Available from: http://www.topuniversities.com/university-rankings-articles/brics-rankings/qs-university-rankings-bricsmethodology.

114. Times Higher Education to Partner with Elsevier on THE World University Rankings [Internet]. Available from: http://www.elsevier.com/about/press-releases/science-and-technology/times-higher-education-to-partner-with-elsevier-on-the-world-university-rankings

115. TES. Our vision [Internet]. TES Global. Available from: http://www.tesglobal.com/.

116. World University Rankings 2013–2014 methodology. *Times Higher Education* [Internet]. [cited April 18, 2015]. Available from: http://www.timeshighereducation.co.uk/world-university-rankings/2013–14/world-ranking/methodology

117. Developing narrative. *Times Higher Education* [Internet]. [cited April 8, 2015]. Available from: http://www.timeshighereducation.co.uk.ezproxy.library.ubc.ca/world-university-rankings/2014/brics-and-emerging-economies/analysis/developing-narrative.

118. Mazrui AA. The African university as a multinational corporation: Problems of penetration and dependency. *Harv Educ Rev*. 1975; 45(2):191.

119. Times Higher Education announces reforms to its World University Rankings [Internet]. *Times Higher Education*. [cited March 6, 2015]. Available from: http://www.timeshighereducation.co.uk.ezproxy.library.ubc.ca/news/times-higher-education-announces-reforms-to-its-world-university-rankings/2017071.article.

120. Fuchs C, Sandoval M. The diamond model of open access publishing: Why policy makers, scholars, universities, libraries, labour unions and the publishing world need to take non-commercial, non-profit open access serious. *Triple C Commun Capital Crit Open Access J Glob Sustain Inf Soc*. 2013; 11(2):428–443.

121. Research Works Act: Elsevier and politicians back down from open-access threat. [Internet]. [cited April 18, 2015]. Available from: http://www.slate.com/blogs/future_tense/2012/02/28/research_works_act_Elsevier_and_politicians_back_down_from_open_access_threat_.html.

122. Feder G, Rohde JE, Sebastian MS, Janlert U, Jimba M, Materia E, et al. Reed Elsevier and the international arms trade. *The Lancet*. 2005; 366(9489):889.

123. Thomson Reuters powers world's university rankings [Internet]. Philadelphia: Thomson Reuters; 2014 Dec. Available from: http://thomsonreuters.com/

en/press-releases/2014/thomson-reuters-powers-worlds-leading-university-rankings.html.

124. About us. | Thomson Reuters [Internet]. [cited April 11, 2015]. Available from: http://thomsonreuters.com/en/about-us.html.

125. Thomson Reuters. InCites™ Overview [Internet]. February 19, 2010 [cited April 11, 2015]. Available from: https://www.youtube.com/watch?v=x03cDnkseM4

126. Phil Baty Biography [Internet]. [cited Retrieved August 19, 2015] Available from: https://www.timeshighereducation.co.uk/content/phil-baty

127. Martin Ince Communications Limited [Internet]. [cited February 26, 2015]. Available from: http://www.martinince.eu/.

128. Your university ranking. Martin Ince Communications [Internet]. [cited April 11, 2015]. Available from: http://www.martinince.eu/ranking/your-university-ranking/.

129. New partner for THE rankings; David Willetts joins TES Global advisory board [Internet]. *Times Higher Education*. November 27, 2014 [cited March 6, 2015]. Available from: http://www.timeshighereducation.co.uk.ezproxy.library.ubc.ca/news/new-partner-for-the-rankings-david-willetts-joins-tes-global-advisory-board/2017164.article.

130. IREG Observatory on Academic Ranking and Excellence. About Us: IREG [Internet]. Available from: http://ireg-observatory.org/en/index.php/about-us

131. International Group Announces Audit of University Rankings – Global – The Chronicle of Higher Education [Internet]. [cited 2014 Oct 30]. Available from: http://chronicle.com.ezproxy.library.ubc.ca/article/International-Group-Announces/124882/

132. QS World University Rankings Approved by IREG [Internet]. Top Universities. [cited 2015 Aug 4]. Available from: http://www.topuniversities.com/university-rankings-articles/world-university-rankings/qs-world-university-rankings-approved-ireg

133. Curtis P, correspondent education. "Trespassing" students defend right to protest. *The Guardian* [Internet]. 2005 Sep 26 [cited 2015 Aug 20]; Available from: http://www.theguardian.com/education/2005/sep/26/students.uk

134. Tang HH. Student political Activism in a global context: An Imperative for enhanced understanding of higher education coordination in Hong Kong. [cited April 27, 2015]; Available from: http://www.researchgate.net/profile/Hei-hang_Hayes_Tang2/publication/269989706_Student_Political_Activism_in_a_Global_Context_An_Analytic_Imperative_for_Enhanced_Understanding_of_Higher_Education_Coordination_in_Hong_Kong/links/549c420d0cf2fedbc30fdaf4.pdf.

135. Palumbo-Liu D. Why is a notorious free-speech censor being given a platform at a major academic gathering? *The Nation* [Internet]. April 23, 2015 [cited June 30, 2015]; Available from: http://www.thenation.com/article/205161/why-notorious-free-speech-censor-being-given-platform-major-academic-gathering.

136. A petition to Monique Canto-Sperber, Ecole Normale Superieure Academic Freedom ENS [Internet]. [cited June 30, 2015]. Available from: https://sites.google.com/site/academicfreedomens/home.

137. Bourdieu P. *On Television and Journalism*. London: Pluto Press; 1998. 112 p.
138. Kress G, Leeuwen TV. Colour as a semiotic mode: notes for a grammar of colour. *Vis Commun*. 2002; 1(3):343–368.
139. Baty P. Top Universities, best of the rest: Under the radar activity – *Times Higher Education* [Internet]. 2011 [cited April 19, 2015]. Available from: http://www.timeshighereducation.co.uk/world-university-rankings/2010–11/world-ranking/analysis/top-universities-400.
140. Baty P. Top universities: With focus, smaller teams can win big – *Times Higher Education* [Internet]. 2011 [cited April 19, 2015]. Available from: http://www.timeshighereducation.co.uk/world-university-rankings/2011–12/world-ranking/analysis/top-universities-200.
141. How to advertise [Internet]. *Times Higher Education*. [cited Oct 29, 2014]. Available from: http://www.timeshighereducation.co.uk/how-to-advertise/.
142. Koller V. `Not just a colour': pink as a gender and sexuality marker in visual communication. *Vis Commun*. 2008; 7(4):395–423.
143. Koh A. The visualization of education policy: a videological analysis of Learning Journeys. *J Educ Policy*. 2009; 24(3):283–315.
144. Times Higher Education. The formula for a world-class university revealed. *Times Higher Education* [Internet]. 2014 [cited April 19, 2015]. Available from: http://www.timeshighereducation.co.uk.ezproxy.library.ubc.ca/world-university-rankings/news/the-formula-for-a-world-class-university-revealed.
145. Agarwal N. That petrol, emotion – *Times Higher Education* [Internet]. 2014 [cited April 19, 2015]. Available from: http://www.timeshighereducation.co.uk/world-university-rankings/2014/reputation-ranking/analysis/that-petrol-emotion.
146. Baty P. Credit check. *Times Higher Education* [Internet]. 2014 [cited April 19, 2015]. Available from: http://www.timeshighereducation.co.uk/world-university-rankings/2014/reputation-ranking/analysis/credit-check.
146. Marginson S. University Rankings and Social Science. *Eur J Educ*. 2014; 49(1):45–59.
148. Baty P. Matter of opinion? Try matter of fact. *Times Higher Education*. 2014; (2142):6–8.
149. Ebb and flow on honour roll. *Times Higher Education* [Internet]. [cited April 13, 2015]. Available from: http://www.timeshighereducation.co.uk/world-university-rankings/2014/reputation-ranking/analysis/ebb-and-flow-on-honour-roll.
150. Ebb and flow | the alternate ebb and flood of the tide [Internet]. [cited April 17, 2015]. Available from: http://www.merriam-webster.com/dictionary/ebb and flow.
151. Creative disrupters are welcome. *Times Higher Education* [Internet]. [cited April 13, 2015]. Available from: http://www.timeshighereducation.co.uk/world-university-rankings/2014/reputation-ranking/analysis/creative-disrupters-are-welcome.
152. Perfect pairings. *Times Higher Education* [Internet]. [cited April 13, 2015]. Available from: http://www.timeshighereducation.co.uk/world-university-rankings/2014/reputation-ranking/analysis/perfect-pairings.
153. Davis G. Excellence in triplicate *Times Higher Education* [Internet]. 2014 [cited April 19, 2015]. Available from: http://www.timeshighereducation.co.uk/

world-university-rankings/2014/reputation-ranking/analysis/excellence-in-triplicate.

154. Peers highlight "valuable contribution" of THE World University Rankings. *Times Higher Education* [Internet]. [cited April 13, 2015]. Available from: http://www.timeshighereducation.co.uk/world-university-rankings/news/house-of-lords-debate.

155. Press AA. Australian universities slip in global reputation rankings. *The Guardian* [Internet]. March 6, 2014 [cited October 29, 2014]; Available from: http://www.theguardian.com/world/2014/mar/06/australian-universities-slip-times-higher-education-rankings.

156. An invitation for the Dublin Young Universities Summit. http://www.cvent.com/events/the-young-universities-summit/

157. Mazawi AE. "'Knowledge Society' or Work as 'Spectacle'? Education for Work and the Prospects of Social Transformation in Arab Societies. Educating a Global Workforce: Knowledge, Knowledge Work, and Knowledge Workers: *World Yearbook of Education*. London: Routledge; 2007. 251–267.

158. Saichaie Kem. Representation on college and university websites: an approach using critical discourse analysis [Internet] [doctoral dissertation, University of Iowa,]. University of Iowa; 2011. Available from: http://ir.uiowa.edu/etd/1071.

159. Canada's International Education Strategy. Harnessing our knowledge advantage to drive innovation and prosperity [Internet]. [cited April 16, 2015]. Available from: http://international.gc.ca/global-markets-marches-mondiaux/education/strategy-strategie.aspx?lang=eng.

160. Canadian Ministers of Education, Imagine Education au/in Canada – Brand Use Guidelines: Home [Internet]. [cited November 22, 2015]. Available from: http://imagine.cmec.ca/en/.

161. Trilokekar RD. IMAGINE: Canada as a leader in international education. How can Canada benefit from the Australian experience? *Can J High Educ.* 2013; 43(2):1–26.

162. Our Place Among the World's Best. The University of British Columbia [Internet]. [cited April 19, 2015]. Available from: http://www.ubc.ca/about/our-place.html.

163. Do L. 2015 Rhodes Scholars: meet Caroline Leps and Moustafa Abdalla | *U of T News* [Internet]. [cited April 19, 2015]. Available from: http://www.news.utoronto.ca/2015-rhodes-scholars-meet-moustafa-abdalla-and-caroline-leps.

164. About us. | *U of T News* [Internet]. [cited April 16, 2015]. Available from: http://news.utoronto.ca/about-us.

165. UBC people | The University of British Columbia [Internet]. [cited April 19, 2015]. Available from: http://www.ubc.ca/about/people.html.

166. Mok KH. Emerging regulatory regionalism in university governance: a comparative study of China and Taiwan. *Glob Soc Educ.* 2010; 8(1):87–103.

167. Mok KH. Marketizing higher education in post-Mao China. *Int J Educ Dev.* 2000; 20(2):109–126.

168. Project 211 and 985.China Education Center [Internet]. [cited April 19, 2015]. Available from: http://www.chinaeducenter.com/en/cedu/cedu-project211.php.

169. Beida vs Tsinghua. China's world class universities and global players [Internet]. The East-West dichotomy. [cited April 16, 2015]. Available from: http://www.east-west-dichotomy.com/beida-vs-tsinghua-chinas-world-class-universities-and-global-players/.

170. Calhoun CJ. *Neither Gods Nor Emperors: Students and the Struggle for Democracy in China.* Berkeley: University of California Press; 1994. 333 p.

171. Government of India. Education statistics at a glance. Ministry of Human Resources Developments Bureau of Planning, Monitoring & Statistics New Delhi; 2014.

172. Agarwal P. *Indian Higher Education Envisioning the Future.* New Delhi; Thousand Oaks, Calif.: SAGE; 2009 [cited April 19, 2015]. Available from: http://public.eblib.com/choice/publicfullrecord.aspx?p=475925.

173. Agarwal P. Higher education in India: The need for change. *Indian Counc Res Int Econ Relat* [Internet]. 2006 [cited January 4, 2015]; Available from: http://dspace.cigilibrary.org/jspui/handle/123456789/20971.

174. Nagaiah K, Srimannarayana G. In defence of the standards of teaching and research in Indian universities in the context of international university rankings. *Curr Sci* 00113891. 2013; http://www.palgraveconnect.com/doifinder/10.1057/9780230306394.

175. Li M, Bray M. Cross-border flows of students for higher education: Push–pull factors and motivations of mainland Chinese students in Hong Kong and Macau. *High Educ.* 2007 Jun; 53(6):791–818.

176. UNESCO. Global Flow of Tertiary-Level Students [Internet]. Institute of Statistics; [cited Oct 30, 2014]. Available from: http://www.uis.unesco.org/Education/Pages/international-student-flow-viz.aspx.

177. Who gets into India's IITs? | The World View | *Inside Higher Education* [Internet]. [cited April 20, 2015]. Available from: https://www.insidehighered.com/blogs/world-view/who-gets-india%E2%80%99s-iits.

178. Why IITB? | IIT Bombay [Internet]. [cited April 16, 2015]. Available from: http://www.iitb.ac.in/en/education/why-iitb.

179 White paper for post-school education and training: Building an expanded and effective and integrated post-school system. South Africa: Department Higher Education and Training; 2013.

180. Walker M. Race is nowhere and race is everywhere: narratives from black and white South African university students in post-apartheid South Africa. *Br J Sociol Educ.* 2005; 26(1):41–54.

181. MacGregor K. South Africa: Student drop-out rates alarming. *University World News.* 2007; (3).

182. Price M. Do university rankings matter? Mail & guardian online. 24 September 2010. http://mg.co.za/article/2010-09-24-do-university-rankings-matter.

183. UCT Archives. UCT shines in World University Ranking by subject [Internet]. 2013. Available from: http://www.researchoffice.uct.ac.za/news/archives/?id=8442&t=dn.

184. UCT. Best-value MBA surges up international ranking [Internet]. 2011. Available from: http://www.uct.ac.za/dailynews/?id=7668.

185. Habib A. Transcending the Past and Reimagining the Future of the South African University' Inaugural Lecture of Professor Adam Habib. 2014; South Africa.

186. Wits and Rankings | Rankings | Strategic Planning Division | About Wits – Wits University [Internet]. [cited April 19, 2015]. Available from: http://www.wits.ac.za/aboutwits/strategicplanningdivision/rankings/15996/wits_and_rankings.html.

187. Lawton D. *The Tory Mind on Education*, 1979–94. London; Washington, D.C: Falmer Press; 1994. 159 p.

188. Education Bill [Bill 137 of 2010–11]. Commons Library Research Paper [Internet]. UK Parliament. [cited April 28, 2015]. Available from: http://www.parliament.uk/briefing-papers/RP11–14/education-bill-bill-137-of-201011.

189. Swain H. Higher education white paper is provoking a winter of discontent [Internet]. *The Guardian*. [cited April 28, 2015]. Available from: http://www.theguardian.com/education/2011/sep/27/higher-education-alternative-white-paper.

190. The impact of research at Russell Group universities [Internet]. 2012 [cited April 19, 2015]. Available from: https://www.youtube.com/watch?v=1oaZ-bhOqJM&feature=youtube_gdata_player.

191. Hazelkorn E. Rankings and the Global Reputation Race. *New Directions for Higher Education*. 2014 Dec 1, 2014 (168):13–26.

192. Eckel P, King J. An Overview of Higher Education in the United States: Diversity, Access and the Role of the Marketplace. American Council on Education; 2004.

193. Shear MD. Colleges rattled as Obama seeks rating system. *The New York Times* [Internet]. May 25, 2014 [cited April 27, 2015]; Available from: http://www.nytimes.com/2014/05/26/us/colleges-rattled-as-obama-presses-rating-system.html.

194. Askehave I. The impact of marketization on higher education genres the international student prospectus as a case in point. *Discourse Stud.* 2007; 9(6):723–742.

195. Fairclough N. *Language and Power*. Longman; 2001. 246 p.

196. Refaie EE. Understanding visual metaphor: the example of newspaper cartoons. *Vis Commun.* 2003 2(1):75–95.

197. Enders J. Branding and ranking in higher education. 2012 [cited January 4, 2015]; Available from: http://doc.utwente.nl/83344/1/EFMD_Z%C3%BCrich_paper_presentation.pdf.

198. Ideland M, Malmberg C. "Our common world" belongs to "Us": constructions of otherness in education for sustainable development. *Crit Stud Educ.* 2014; 55(3):369–386.

199. Sidhu R. Educational Brokers in Global Education Markets. *J Stud Int Educ.* 2002; 6(1):16–43.

200. Naidoo R, Shankar A, Veer E. The consumerist turn in higher education: Policy aspirations and outcomes. *Journal of Marketing Management.* 2011 Oct 1, 27(11–12):1142–62.

201. Chan AS, Fisher D. *The Exchange University: Corporatization of Academic Culture*. UBC Press; 2008. 244 p.

202. Habermas J. The *Theory of Communicative Action*. Boston: Beacon Press; 1984. 2 p.

203. Giacalone RA. Academic rankings in research institutions: A case of skewed mind-sets and professional amnesia. *Acad Manag Learn Educ.* 2009; 8(1):122–126.
204. Cramer KM, Page S. Calibrating Canadian universities: Rankings for sale once again. *Can J Sch Psychol.* 2007; 22(1):4–13.
205. Badat S. The world-class university and the global south. *World Social Science Report* 2010: Knowledge Divides. UNESCO; International Social Science Council; 2010. p. 245–247.
206. Vostal F, Robertson S. Knowledge mediators and lubricating channels: On the temporal politics of remissioning the university. TOPIA *Can J Cult Stud* [Internet]. 2012 [cited March 24, 2015]; 1(28). Available from: http://pi.library.yorku.ca.ezproxy.library.ubc.ca/ojs/index.php/topia/article/view/36203.
207. Amid boycott, Elsevier backtracks on research bill [Internet]. [cited April 21, 2015]. Available from: http://www.cbc.ca/1.1251410.
208. Santos B. Beyond abyssal thinking: From global lines to ecologies of knowledge. *Eurozine.* 2007.
209. Andreotti V, Ahenakew C, Cooper G. Epistemological pluralism: Ethical and pedagogical challenges in higher education. *Altern Int J Indig Peoples* [Internet]. May 13, 2011 [cited April 20, 2015]; 7(1). Available from: http://www.content.alternative.ac.nz/index.php/alternative/article/view/61.
210. Brass K, Rowe D. Knowledge limited: Public communication, risk and university media policy. *Continuum.* 2009; 23(1):53–76.
211. Pauwels L. A multimodal framework for analyzing websites as cultural expressions. *J Comput Commun.* 2012.
212. Gill H, Purru K, Lin. In the midst of participatory action research practices: Moving towards decolonizing and decolonial praxis. *Reconceptualizing Educ Res Methodol.* 2012; 3(1):1–15.
213. Burch P. Hidden markets: *The New Education Privatization.* New York: Routledge; 2009. 181 p.
214. Stack, M. The Times Higher Education ranking product: visualising excellence through media. *Globalisation, Societies and Education.* November 2013; 11(4):560–582.

Index